Self-Renewal

HIGH PERFORMANCE IN A HIGH-STRESS WORLD

Dennis Jaffe, Ph.D.
Cynthia Scott, Ph.D., M.P.H.

CRISP PUBLICATIONS, INC.
Menlo Park, California

HIGH PERFORMANCE IN A HIGH-STRESS WORLD

Editor: Beverly Manber
Cover and Interior Design: Interface Studios
Layout and Composition: Interface Studios
Managing Editor: Kathleen Barcos

Crisp Publications, Inc.
Menlo Park, California

Library of Congress Catalog Card Number 93-72971
Jaffe, Dennis and Scott, Cynthia
Self-Renewal
ISBN 1-56052-265-8

PREFACE

This book requires your participation. Each chapter helps you understand one dimension of self-management or self-renewal, and offers concrete steps you can take to achieve each of them. You need to be willing to experiment, to take risks and to try new things. This process of change may have profound effects on your life and work.

The end of the book contains self-assessment questions that ask you to explore facets of your life. Each assessment will help you gather information about whether some dimensions of your life and your way of managing pressure cause you difficulty and contribute to burnout.

Begin by skimming the book, identifying the sections that seem most critical or important to you. The chapters can be read in any order. One way to know if a chapter is particularly relevant to you is to try the self-assessment exercises at the end of the book. If you come out with a score that indicates you need to work in a particular area; read the chapter that corresponds to that exercise.

Do the exercises, and work through the material in each chapter in short study periods of a half hour to an hour. Set aside a little time each day to work on personal change. If you take special time and ask not to be interrupted, you will show yourself that you take this work, and yourself, seriously. You will make a commitment to change. Changes do not occur overnight. They demand work, practice, self-reflection and dedication.

This book is organized into three parts. Part I, **Managing Change and Creating Personal Power**, explores the ways you can create more effective responses to your daily demands, changes and pressures. The chapters in this section explore the pressures, demands and changes in life, and the internal and external strategies you can use to manage yourself most effectively. Skills for attaining personal power and active, helpful coping strategies are outlined.

Part II, **Sharing and Connecting**, is about getting help and support from the people around you—at home, at work and in the community. It is about connecting to others and creating positive, helpful, self-supporting relationships.

Part III, **Renewing Yourself**, shifts the focus back to you. Using self-renewal techniques to become aware of your inner self and its complex structure, you will find ways to take better care of yourself.

Contents

Introduction

INTRODUCTION

The working person of yesterday was most likely concerned with direct production. He or she worked on the farm, at home, in a shop or factory. Today, the majority of workers are concerned with information and service. People work with customers or clients, transferring information, preparing reports and often interacting intensely with each other. This new environment demands vast new sets of skills. Instead of physical stamina and routine tasks, today we are presented with multiple demands, many choices and decisions, and a world in which we need to work together on complex tasks. Instead of physical activity, the primary demands are mental and interpersonal.

At work and in our personal lives, many people find themselves feeling overwhelmed and struggling to get things under control. They feel pressured by time and continually need to respond and act, often without having a clear idea of the outcome. Life is made up of pressures and uncertainty, to which we need to adapt.

People respond to the modern world with bodies and minds that were designed to function well in a far simpler world. Our primary mental and physical characteristics evolved several million years ago, whereas the world we inhabit today was created by us less than a generation ago. The things that we demand of ourselves are not the things we were designed to do. As a result, we fall prey to all forms of physical and emotional illness and distress, and we experience difficulty and distress with the life we lead. Many people use the term *burnout* to refer to a generalized depletion of energy, lack of involvement and inability to function well and to achieve satisfaction. Many people feel tired and helpless to do anything to overcome it.

There must be a better way, we think to ourselves.

- How can we cope with the pressures of our work and our lives?
- Is it possible to preserve ourselves from illness and distress?
- How can we perform our jobs effectively and meet the demands upon us?

In the traditional view, the person was primarily reactive, responding reflexively and automatically to pressures and demands. The person was primarily determined by the circumstances of his or her life; to live well, he or she merely had to continue offering the correct responses to the environment, which was also predictable and regular. Today, the environment has been changed, and we need to respond by changing ourselves.

The new, emerging view of the person begins with the observation that, in addition to reacting to pressures and demands, we have the ability to modify ourselves and respond to demands in creative and novel ways. The human being, unlike a machine or most other forms of life, can reorganize in response to pressure and change. When pressures build up, instead of reacting to them one at a time, we have the capacity to plan, to consider alternatives and to attempt something completely new and different.

The new view of the person emphasizes the unique human ability to be creative, to adapt by reorganizing and redefining the situation and to become self-determining. Instead of giving up or giving in to daily pressures, we can evolve and adapt.

Many people today seek some form of training in various aspects of life-management. They attend seminars or read books about self-regulation techniques, life planning, time management, positive thinking, etc. With this guidance, people expect to learn how to overcome self-created pain and distress, master their lives and realize their potentials.

This vast array of workshops presents common themes and techniques. They emphasize increasing self-awareness, taking responsibility for life choices, clarifying needs and intentions in situations, increasing personal risks, modifying self-defeating patterns of thought and action, and actively responding to demands.

The central message of this book is that in our complex and demanding world, people need to learn how to manage, maintain and renew themselves. These skills are as essential to self-preservation and effective work performance as the traditional skills of managing people and resources outside of oneself. Traditional management training and organizational practices have for too long neglected the needs of the individual and neglected teaching people to be sensitive to themselves. As a result, signs and symptoms of burnout are epidemic.

This book is designed to help you respond creatively to the pressure and demands of your work and your life. The goal is to keep you healthy and to avoid your getting burned out from life stress. It will help you perform up to your capacity and achive your personal level of *peak performance*. You can learn those skills through a process of self-exploration. At each step of the way you will look at various aspects of your life and work, and assess the effectiveness of your functioning. Then you will learn how to respond creatively.

Learning new ways involves three types of activity:

Self-awareness: A close look at what you are currently doing and rethinking of those responses. Ask yourself critically why you are doing certain things and what effects these actions bring.

Self-renewal: The inner exploration of the effects of your behavior on your body and your psyche, and the conscious regular attempts to rejuvenate and regenerate yourself.

Self-management: Begin to consciously determine your strategies in response to daily pressures of work and personal life.

THE THREAT OF STRESS

A few decades ago, if you asked someone what causes disease, he or she would have answered, "germs." Today, a more common answer would be "stress." Stress is blamed for everything, and is considered an evil with which we all live. The truth is that while stress may be involved in the creation of many modern forms of illness and distress, the stress response within our body is actually our primary protector, a mechanism that can be mobilized to preserve or to harm us. Stress can be our protector as well as our destroyer.

The word "stress" was coined in 1946 by Hans Selye, who spent his life looking at the general ways that the body protects itself against difficulty and danger. According to Selye, stress is:

The nonspecific response of the body to any demand placed upon it. . . . All agents and changes to which we are exposed produce a nonspecific increase in the need to perform adaptive functions and thereby to establish normalcy. . . . It is immaterial whether the agent or situation we face is pleasant or unpleasant; all that counts is the intensity of the demand for readjustment or adaptation.

The stress response is then, our body's response to any change, demand, pressure or threat from the outside. The stress response aims to bring the agitated or disturbed body back to normal and to enable it to protect itself from the external situation.

The demand to adapt comes from the continuing pressures of our work or our families and the internal pressures and demands we make on ourselves. The stress response is an ally whose goal is to keep us together physically and emotionally. Our lives are a continuing struggle against demands, which can spur us to creative achievements, provide us with excitement or burn us out in bitterness, apathy and frustration.

However, it is the same demands that cause the stress response in our body to protect us, that does us in?

It's often the sheer number of demands which is more than we can handle. For example:

- We are assaulted by noise, cars, pollution and the threat of crime or accident.

- The staggering pace of change in our world.

- Employees are overloaded, pressured or frustrated.

- In personal relationships, our needs are not always met.

The stress response is the emotional and physical reaction that the body makes to each of these demands and changes. The body reacts the same way whether the demand is emotional—pressure to complete a job, conflict in a relationship—or physical—a car swerving at you, a mugger threatening you. No matter what the demand, the body mobilizes for physical action.

Most of the demands we face do not require quick, decisive physical action. Therefore, although the body is aroused for action many times a day, because the pressures are emotional or psychological we inhibit the body's natural responses. This creates muscle tension, headaches, stomach cramps and some of the more serious, stress-related physical symptoms.

By not responding to demands physically, and by poor management of the work and other pressures, we keep ourselves in a continual state of physical arousal. The negative physical effects are due to inadequate, delayed, misplaced or inhibited responses to pressure. The pressure is never released, so tension builds up cumulatively. Just like a car engine that's run when it is not in gear, or a toaster that is left on, our bodies burn out. To gain control over this negative cycle, we need to cultivate the skills of **self-awareness**, **self-renewal** and **self-management.**

THE EFFECTS OF STRESS

All around us we can see people struggling ineffectively with stress, pressure and tension. Smoking, drinking, drug use and overeating are all ineffective responses to life stress. These form our major public health hazards and indirectly, in the form of accidents and impaired work performance, lead to inestimable harm and cost.

There are short-term and long-term effects of our inability to manage stress effectively. Each day's frustrations, struggles and difficulties lead to minor symptoms, pains and emotional distress. These tensions cause distress, and we try a variety of effective and ineffective strategies to deal with them.

Over longer periods chronic daily stresses wear us down, causing more severe problems. As tension builds up, we may fruitlessly begin smoking, drinking, eating too much or depending on some other form of addiction that carries with it its own negative effects. Ironically, many of our most severe health problems and social problems stem from our own ineffective attempts to find relief from the tension of everyday stress. Serious illness can result from long-term stress or from self-defeating methods of managing it.

Emotional and psychological distress is debilitating and it takes an increasing human toll. The incidence of chronic depression and anxiety is rising, suggesting that these emotional states are one long-term result of daily stress. The following symptoms stem from an inability to manage stress:

- Marital difficulties
- Antisocial behavior
- Child and spouse abuse
- Interpersonal conflict

Finally, the loss of meaning, commitment and connection to work, family or life tasks—i.e., "burnout"—is increasing. In short, the daily stress is slowly using up people, resulting in many of the serious social and health problems that our society faces.

THE STRESS CYCLE

In popular usage, stress refers to both demanding activities as well as the feelings that result from these activities. Thus, stress refers to both the cause and the effect, suggesting that the two are so closely linked that it is hard to separate stimulus from response. This is important.

To clarify how the stress process takes place, it is necessary to outline the entire chain of events within us that produces it. Things can be done at each step that can reduce the negative or dysfunctional effects.

STRESSORS: THE TRIGGER

All of the external pressures, demands, threats, changes, conflicts, challenges and difficulties we face can trigger our body's stress response. Anything that happens in our world that demands some change, adjustment or response from us is termed a *stressor*. To protect us, our body responds to almost anything, at the slightest hint something is wrong or that our reserves of energy will be needed.

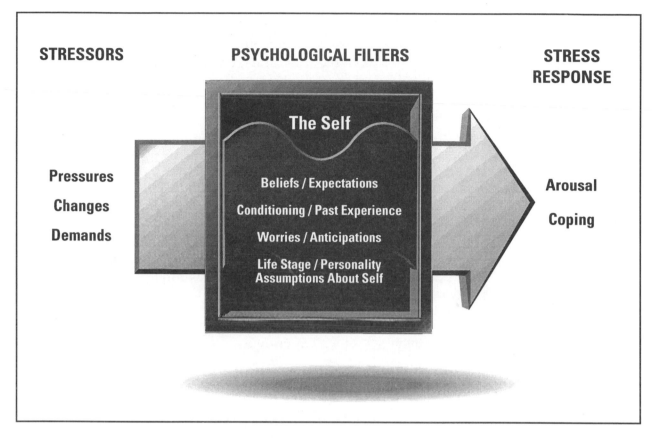

STRESSORS

Pressures

Changes

Demands

PSYCHOLOGICAL FILTERS

The Self

Beliefs / Expectations

Conditioning / Past Experience

Worries / Anticipations

Life Stage / Personality
Assumptions About Self

STRESS RESPONSE

Arousal

Coping

Figure 1-1: TRIGGERING THE STRESS RESPONSE

Familiar stressors include:

- Any life change or important life event
- Threats to our person or self-esteem
- Loss of someone or something we care for or depend on
- Conflicting or ambiguous demands or expectations
- Pressure of deadlines, too much work and confused priorities
- Conflicts or difficulties with other people
- Frustration or threats to our personal needs

Each individual finds some stressors more difficult or demanding than others; that has to do with our personal style and background. Everyone can list scores of common stressors in his or her daily life. However, when we experience several pressures at once, or if a pressure is especially severe, our stress level increases and we are at risk of illness or personal crisis.

Evaluating the Threat

To a degree, stress is manufactured within our minds. To experience stress, the mind must consider a situation threatening or difficult. For example, if two people are given the same task, one might feel his job is on the line or have grave doubts about his ability; the other, with the same ability and standing within the organization, might feel comfortable with herself and her job standing. The first person would perceive the task as more stressful.

People manufacture stress for themselves when they worry, anticipate the worst or create unrealistic demands on themselves. When we imagine a stressful situation, our body acts as if the event is really happening, which triggers the stress response. We can reduce stress simply by reducing the amount of negative thinking.

Childhood learning creates several factors that determine how much stress we experience.

- Feelings about ourselves
- Feelings about our abilities
- Expectations of ourselves
- Expectations of other people

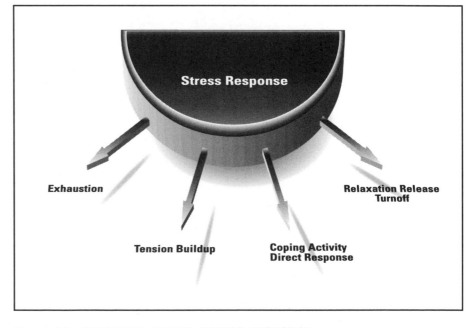

Figure 1-2: OUTCOMES OF THE STRESS RESPONSE

Each person learns a style of responding to challenges and thinking about the world that greatly affects how safe or threatening the world appears to him or her. A person who feels safe and confident will experience less stress than one who is fearful and full of self-doubt.

THE STRESS RESPONSE

Regardless of the stressor and of our evaluation of it, when we perceive something as even mildly stressful, our entire body swings into immediate action. The muscles tighten, the brain sends signals to release adrenaline into the bloodstream, blood vessels constrict, the stomach tightens and secretes acid, breathing becomes quick and shallow, and we experience intense emotions such as rage, fear, anger and anxiety. This integrated response to threat, which evolved eons ago to allow us to mobilize the tremendous energy needed for survival in a world of predators, can be as much of a problem as a protector.

Many situations trigger unnecessary stress. We do not always need the physical arousal and mobilization of energy of this powerful reaction. Thus, for many situations, we need to learn to train ourselves to either avoid activating the stress response in the first place or else, once activated, learn to turn it off. Otherwise we will literally burn ourselves out. The feelings of exhaustion, depletion, muscle tension and depression are often signs that we have repeatedly aroused ourselves via the stress response with no release.

Turning Off

While there are many ways to turn on the stress response, there are relatively few methods to turn it off. We can turn off the physical response by taking direct, physical action against the situation or threat. Early in human evolution, this meant fighting or fleeing; hence the term *fight/flight reaction* is often used for the first stage of the stress response.

In most contemporary situations, we can turn off the stress response by actively responding to a situation or by physically exercising the stress out of our body. Quiet forms of relaxation can be used to activate an opposite response in the body—the relaxation response. Techniques such as meditation, progressive relaxation, guided imagery, biofeedback and self-hypnosis can all activate this opposing psychophysiological state.

TENSION: THE PATHWAY TO ILLNESS AND DISTRESS

What we commonly refer to as stress is more properly labeled *tension*. Tension is the buildup of unrelieved stress within our bodies. We experience tension as tightened muscles, aches and pains, upset stomach, anxiety or depression, feelings of depletion or lack of energy, emotional burnout, withdrawal and conflict in relationships. These symptoms crop up when we react repeatedly to stress without effectively managing it. Tension is the residue that is left when we:

- Feel we cannot do something about the stress we are under
- Fail to do something about it
- Fail to acknowledge its existence

Over time, tension signals that our body has worn down. Illness, in the form of physical or emotional breakdown, is the final result.

Coping: Self-Management of Stress

People learn functional and dysfunctional ways of managing tension. Functional tension management includes exercise, relaxation, sharing it with others, hobbies and diversions. Dysfunctional methods include denying, eating, drinking, smoking, drug use and withdrawal.

Each person develops a coping style—general patterns of reacting to stressful situations. These patterns include thoughts, expectations, emotions and behavior in response to stressors and to tension. Some common patterns of coping with stress seem to lead more frequently to illness and difficulty than others. Rooted in personality, these coping styles are a set of habits that can be modified and changed. Therefore, our stress levels are, in large part, under our control.

In looking at the whole stress cycle, a person has several clear avenues to reduce his or her stress level, or to manage the stress more effectively:

- Reduce the pressure or demands from the environment.
- Modify negative, self-critical, self-defeating or other mental patterns that create or amplify threats or dangers.

- Cope actively and effectively with demands and situations that trigger the stress response.
- Create supportive, intimate and work relationships.
- Practice effective techniques of tension management to avoid the negative effects of disabling tension buildup.

STRESS AND HEALTH

Everything we do, and everything we feel and experience, influences our health. For example, researchers have found that people are more likely to become ill under any of the following conditions:

- Experiencing many changes—good or bad—in your life
- Losing a spouse or someone you love
- Not feeling connected to other people
- Holding in feelings of anger and resentment
- Pushing yourself without taking time to rest
- Feeling helpless and not in control

These things happen to all of us at one time or another. So what can a person do to remain well?

It helps to be aware of the connection between stress and illness. You need to take care of yourself when you know you are under stress that may lead to illness. There is evidence that illness and physical symptoms come about when we ignore our body's subtle and gentle warnings.

The key to managing or holding off the breakdown of our bodies is not simply traditional medicine or health insurance; it lies in preventing damage from occurring for as long as possible. We all need to practice preventive health care, ecause once an organ deteriorates, the rest of the body follows. In addition, as we live longer, preventive medicine may make the difference between a disabled and painful life or a vital and productive life. Furthermore, an emerging concensus among health leaders is that preventive medicine that emphasizes selfcare is the major medical resource of the future. Over time, the quality of life becomes an important factor—mere survival is not enough.

SELF-MANAGEMENT AND SELF-RENEWAL

The president of a manufacturing firm manages many resources, organizes scores of people in complex tasks, and exerts control over a vast system that brings in materials, transforms them into products and extends into the community through sales and marketing. With all this power, he feels helpless, frustrated and out of control when he develops chronic migraine headaches, elevated blood pressure and periodic stomach trouble.

He seeks help from a physician who prescribes several types of medication to loosen the constriction in his head, to ease the pressure in his circulatory system and to diminish his stomach's secretion of hormones. The medical solution to his physical problems has certain consequences. The medications have long-term effects on his body that create further difficulties; with continued use, some medicines lose their effectiveness. More importantly, the reasons behind his symptoms remain a mystery. Why does his head hurt and his stomach tighten when there are problems at the plant? If he seeks only a medical solution he will leave untouched the underlying conditions in his life that may be creating the symptoms.

This businessman wants to know whether his symptoms are *caused* by stress. He has learned to divide the world of health into two camps: *real* physical illnesses, and psychosomatic illnesses that are due to various kinds of emotional stress. Actually, there is no dividing line. No matter what the ailment, all difficulties are affected and often triggered by stress.

For example, heart disease is due to many factors, all of which put strain on the circulatory system. These factors include heredity, diet and sometimes lack of proper exercise and the presence of chronic stress. If a business disaster triggers a heart attack, was stress the *cause* of it? Yes and no; it was one of several causes. A change in any one of the factors might make the body much more able to resist the stress of the disaster.

For this businessman's ailment, medical treatment is only one part of health care. How can this man, who is able to manage his external world, coordinate people and products, be unable to control his health?

In the past there were good reasons for not extending our mastery to our inner worlds. But the medical problems we all face today cannot be overcome without lifting the veil that separates us from awareness and management of our physical environment and our psychological body processes.

Anyone who can manage other people has all the abilities and qualifications for self-management. A person who decides that his health and well-being are too important to be left solely in the hands of a physician, will discover new possibilities.

- He can look inward and listen to his body, becoming more sensitive to its needs
- He can learn that his body *can* withstand an intense and difficult lifestyle.
- He can explore ways to manage internal physical processes, like lowering his blood pressure
- He can regulate his activities to attain the most effective organization and improve his own health. In short, he can recognize his stress symptoms and respond creatively.

PEAK PERFORMANCE

Stress is associated not only with distress, but also with excitement, achievement and effective organization. In a study of major corporate leaders' attitudes toward stress, Herbert Benson found that many of them felt that creating stress and pressure in their organization was an important factor in creating effectiveness. They felt that they thrived on the challenge of stress, and they instilled that pressure and challenge in their employees.

Like many commonsense insights, the association of stress with optimal performance is partly correct and partly incorrect. It is true, for example, that positive stress is something that many people seek—excitement, risk, thrills, challenge, competition and overcoming adversity. All of these positive stresses give our life flavor and meaning, and spur us on to important, creative and satisfactory achievement. Stress-seeking is a quality that helps account for human beings' remarkable adaptiveness and accomplishments.

Yet, each person seems to have a line where challenge becomes burden and excitement becomes fear. Hans Selye talks about individual differences in relation to stress. Some people, he notes, are turtles: they need a steady, predictable environment in which to shine. Others, including most corporate chiefs, are racehorses: they need a high level of stimulation, challenge and change to bring out their best. The mistake is thinking that one climate serves all.

Peak performance takes place for each person at a certain level of stress or pressure. If there is too little stress, things are boring and there is an underload. If there is too much stress, burnout or overload diminishes performance. The determination of each person's optimal stress level, and the creation of an environment that supports it, is an important aspect of effective stress management.

As we can see from the Performance Curve (Figure 1-3), there is an optimal level of stress for each person, at which he

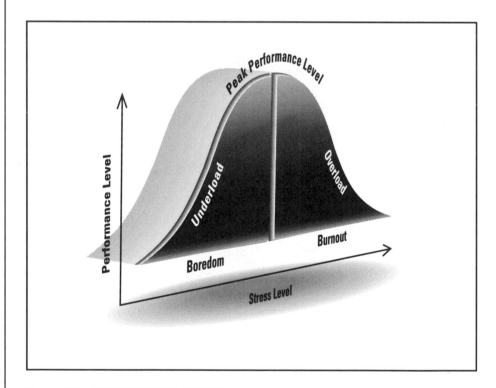

Figure 1-3: PERFORMANCE CURVE

or she reaches peak performance. Effectiveness drops off with either too much or too little stress or pressure. Things can become too dull, just as they can become too stimulating. The task for each person, and for an organization as a whole, is to discover this optimal level.

Remember some times when you were working at your best, when you were involved, challenged and excited. Summon as much detail as possible. Now, answer the following questions.

EXERCISE 1

- What are the qualities of your environment?
- What sorts of pressures or deadlines spur you to action?
- What tasks energize you?
- Which ones bore you?
- Do you work best alone or with others?
- What type of help or guidance do you need?

RESPONDING TO STRESS

Figure 1-4 (see page 18) illustrates two broad styles of responses a person can make to the daily pressures of life.

Defensive path: This person remains unaware and unreflective concerning the effects of stress and his or her ways of responding to it. This path is characterized by denial and avoidance of the effects of one's behavior and the effects of stress on oneself. Characteristic responses to stress are reactive, consisting mainly of reflexes, methods of coping that were primarily learned early in life. Over time, these ineffective responses lead to illness, distress, emotional and physical breakdown.

Creative path: This person utilizes self-awareness, the techniques of self-renewal and the skills of self-management. This person moves in the direction of peak performance and remains in balance in his or her life. Responding creatively, the person combines self-care with the proper skills to complete tasks.

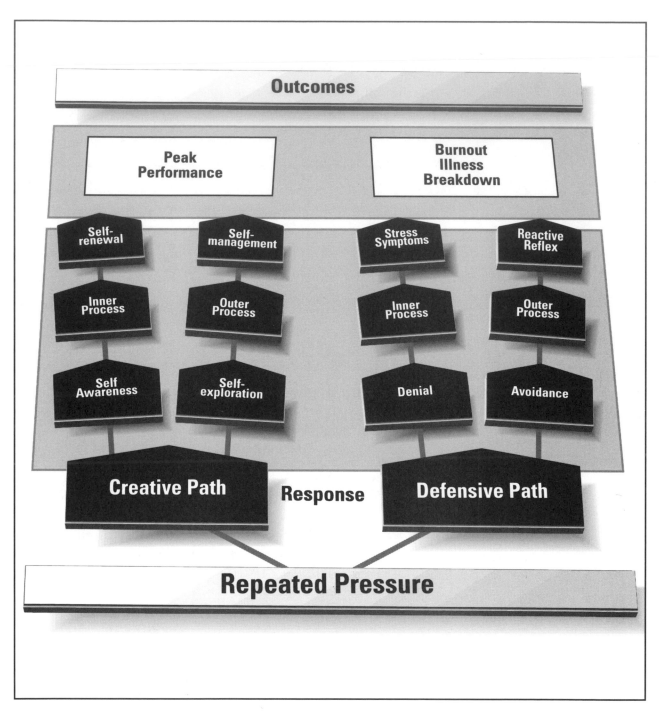

Figure 1-4: CREATIVE AND DEFENSIVE RESPONSES TO STRESS AND THEIR OUTCOMES

GUIDELINES FOR CHANGING

Certain general principles apply to all efforts of personal change. Representative of experiences of people who have changed many aspects of their lives, these guidelines should be applied as follows:

Make changes in small steps. If you try to change everything at once, you feel helpless and overwhelmed. Think about what you want to change, and select a small but significant first step.

Change one thing at a time. Changing demands careful attention to one's goals. Then, use the good feelings and success achieved in one area to help you scale the more difficult heights. Begin with the types of change you are most likely to be able to make or which you expect to be the most pleasurable for you.

Have clear, concrete, specific goals. Telling yourself you want to deal better with stress is vague and confusing. Give yourself a clear, concrete vision of what you want to achieve. List the specifics of what you want to change.

Be aware of how you are when you begin. Our general ideas of how we react to stress may be quite different from the reality. Before you begin to change, you need to be aware of current patterns. Do this by keeping a record of the type of behavior you wish to change. Your behavior patterns may not be as bad as you think, or you may have an even greater problem than you believe. Either way, it is important to know.

Offer rewards. If you offer yourself rewards each time you meet a goal, you will be more likely to feel good about yourself and persevere. Being nice to yourself is what self-renewal is all about.

Find a support person. It is hard for a single member of a family to change any habit if the others are not encouraging and supportive. The most effective change program is one where you have a buddy whose job is to encourage you, check up on you, and share activities with you. If your buddy is trying to make similar changes in his or her life, the partnership is even better.

Expect failures and relapses. We all experience failure. But failure is a matter of degree. Change is always a matter of ups and downs, not a smooth course. You can help yourself by expecting to encounter difficulty and have relapses. You can help yourself by planning days off on weekends or by picking yourself up if you veered from your plan and getting back on course. A slight relapse need not divert you from your overall goal, and you will find that flexibility does not cause you to lose sight of, or lose your ability to achieve, your goals.

Use positive imagery and self-talk. You can encourage or discourage yourself by the way you talk and think. In a positive peak performance program we need to give ourselves a constant diet of positive suggestions and encouragement, and continually imagine how we will feel, look and act when we are healthy. Use positive mental imagery to program your mental attitudes, which in turn are linked to habitual behavior.

MANAGING CHANGE AND CREATING PERSONAL POWER

Chapter One

HOW WE CREATE PRESSURE

**STRESSORS:
THE PULL
OF THE
ENVIRONMENT**

Take a few moments to remember some of the recent situations you found demanding or difficult. What made them stressful?

Everything that seems stressful to us involves a change or event that demands a corresponding response. When a co-worker is absent, the event is stressful if you are forced to adjust your workload accordingly. When somebody seems to challenge your competence or ability, the stress-provoking demand is for you to prove yourself.

Our lives are composed of thousands of demands, pressures and changes that force us to adapt and change many times a day. The pace of change in our lives and the multiple sources of pressure upon us make modern life uniquely stressful.

Added to that is the continual assault on our senses. Noise, traffic, poor air and a crush of people can overload our nervous system. The more stresses, the less we are able to cope.

We pay a price for living in a free, loosely regulated society. The pressure of making the right choice among so many offered and the uncertainty of jobs and relationships mean that many of us cannot let down our guards and feel safe. Conflict, is also a part of our lives. At home and at work the pressure of angry demands, needs and expectations of other people wear us out. It often seems as if getting things for ourselves can come only at the expense of somebody else, or through conflict.

When we look more closely at the pressures and demands on us we see that the picture is incomplete. Pressure is not just something that is done to us. Rather it results from us interacting with our environment. Being asked to do something is not necessarily a demand or pressure, nor is this necessarily stressful to us. We can ignore the request, or we can welcome it as a recognition of our worth. If we experience the request in either of these ways, we will feel only a slight pressure. But suppose we see a request as a test of our ability and feel that a job, a course grade or a friendship is at stake. Then the pressure mounts. For many, pressure stems from our preception of demands we face.

For this reason, it is hard to categorize events and situations according to their degree of stressfulness. Pressure is a consequence of the demands and changes, our preception of them and our reaction to them. The measurement of our stress and of how much pressure there is in our lives is highly subjective.

The exercises and inventories in this chapter will help you diagnose your **personal stress level**. You will look at the various pressures, changes, demands and stressful events that occur in your life and explore which of them create the most pressure.

If burnout is the outcome of poor management of your life, the way you allow yourself to become pressured, distressed and upset is an important starting point to overcome it. Stressors lie in the interaction between you and the world.

SOURCES OF STRESS

Many of us see pressures and demands as one big sticky mass, without shape or form. Each added incident seems to stick along with the whole. While things may *feel* that way, this view leaves us feeling overwhelmed and helpless. What can we do, we ask ourselves, since the mass is just too large to budge?

In fact, our stressors—pressures, demands and changes—have a structure and pattern. Specific types of pressure predominate, and we can take steps to manage each appropriately and effectively. The first step is to recognize your own paricular types of pressure.

We can divide the stressors in our lives into two broad categories:

Chronic, ongoing stressors: daily hassles and irritating, frustrating, depressing and upsetting incidents that occur regularly in our lives. These take place at work, at home, in the community and in our relationships. They include small, predictable things like traffic jams, and ongoing pressures like excessive demands for work performance.

Episodic stressors: the crises, changes, unplanned incidents and planned transitions that take us from one life situation to another and demand adjustment and coping.

The distinction between ongoing and episodic stressors is important. First, it is important to know whether the pressures you face are due to particular crises that are time-limited, and can be overcome, or are regular parts of your life. The process of coping with chronic, ongoing stressors is different from coping with discrete crises. An ongoing stressor usually cannot be overcome; it must be met and managed in a self-supportive way. If you cannot stop the demands of a job or of your daily commute, you need to find ways to manage your responses to the demands and the traffic to preserve your well-being.

We are always under the spell of many chronic, ongoing stressors and, much of the time, some episodic incidents and changes as well. Sometimes it is not the particular changes, but the cumulative effect of one on top of another that leaves us feeling burned and drained.

The four boxes in Exercise 2 represent the two categories of stressors, and our work and personal world—two major settings where stress occurs.

- Think of the various sources and types of stressors that you are experiencing in your life right now.
- Write them in the appropriate boxes and underline those that are the most pressing, severe or difficult for you to manage.

A clear picture will begin to emerge of the major sources of stress in your life, whether they are chronic or result from episodic changes or crises that you might overcome and adjust to.

SETTINGS FOR STRESS

Most of us can single out our work or our family as the major source of our problems. An unfortunate few feel that their stress arises in both settings.

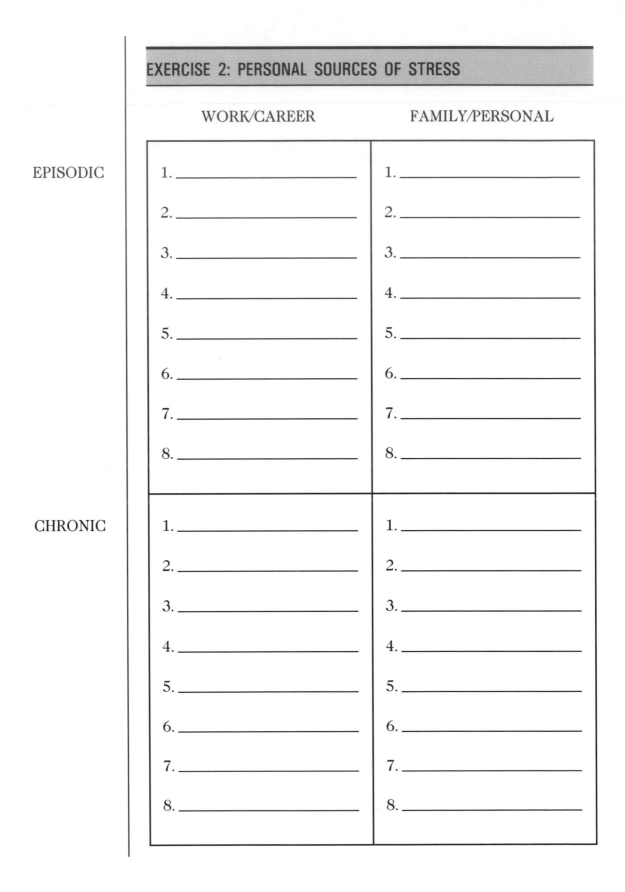

EXERCISE 2: PERSONAL SOURCES OF STRESS

	WORK/CAREER	FAMILY/PERSONAL
EPISODIC	1. _____	1. _____
	2. _____	2. _____
	3. _____	3. _____
	4. _____	4. _____
	5. _____	5. _____
	6. _____	6. _____
	7. _____	7. _____
	8. _____	8. _____
CHRONIC	1. _____	1. _____
	2. _____	2. _____
	3. _____	3. _____
	4. _____	4. _____
	5. _____	5. _____
	6. _____	6. _____
	7. _____	7. _____
	8. _____	8. _____

There really is no way to compare the actual degree of stress different people experience. Everyone's stress feels big. The important question is not the quantity of your stress, but rather its effects on your body and your life.

For Exercise 3 turn to Assessment 1 in the Appendix. For each statement, estimate how much pressure it adds to your life. When you have completed the scale, you will have some sense of the patterns of your stress. These patterns are the places to focus your attention when you begin to think about making changes.

Job Stress

Our perceptions of stress on the job are usually hampered by outmoded, mechanistic conceptions of work and organizations. The misconception is that the organization is a firmly defined, almost solid structure, consisting of jobs that are specified by role slots, all connected into sections, work groups and divisions. People are expected to fit into defined jobs and to conform their behavior to what is expected. The organization is inflexible and difficult, if not impossible, to change. We expect to feel resentful and alienated from such a self-limiting and constricting situation.

New visions of jobs and organizations have emerged that offer more realistic perceptions of the person and the organization. In these newer views, the organization is seen as a web of fluid alliances that shifts to accommodate new energy and people. People and organizations are organic wholes. The organization and the job role are not as firmly fixed or clearly defined. They represent a human network, organized around central goals, cultural norms, values and pathways toward these goals. The human being has more power, meaning and influence over the organization.

We all experience job stress. We feel it in our bodies, in our feelings, in our energy levels and in our responses to our work. We are familiar with these reactions. But we need to step back a bit to understand more clearly how the stress arises from our interaction with our work setting.

For Exercise 4, turn to Assessment 2 in the Appendix. For each job-related stressor, indicate how often you feel that way or have that sense or experience.

Relating to Job Stress

We are not robots who are forced into job slots that pressure us, alienate us and eventually burn us out, when we are exchanged for another worker. On the contrary, the way to look at job stress is as a result of our personal interaction with our job and organization. Work is a situation where we negotiate, make requests and undertake tasks for other people. Job stress results from many discrete, particular situations and procedures. Some are within our control and, once noticed, can be changed through negotiation and interaction; others are less controllable.

The first step in dealing with life stress is to break it down into its stressors. Stressors force us to adjust or respond to them. Whether the demand is one we make on ourselves—such as an internal pressure to excel—or one that comes from the environment—such as competition with a co-worker for a promotion—our body triggers a psychophysiological stress response to each of these situations. Therefore, stressors demand that we exercise effective external and internal management. We call this self-management of our response to the situation and self-renewal in response to the needs of our body for care.

As human beings, we face challenges to our physical well-being, as well as challenges to our emotional well-being and self-esteem. Pressures and demands become stressful because we have to respond while maintaining our well-being and self-esteem against both real and potential threats.

While any external change or demand can be perceived as a source of stress, the majority of our life stresses fall into several categories:

Loss: The loss (or threat of loss) of someone or something we are attached to is painful. We need to go through a period of mourning, sadness or depression while making adjustments in our lives.

Threat: The resulting stress response in our body is the same whether the threat is to our self-esteem or to our person.

Frustration: We experience frustration when anyone or anything even potentially seems to prevent us from meeting our basic needs or getting what we want. We feel the most stress when something blocks our path and we feel helpless to change it.

Uncertainty: A potential threat, loss, harm or frustration can be especially stressful. Our imaginations help us to be creative; they also allow us to worry about and anticipate all manner of disasters. To our bodies, the imagined danger and reality are the same: the stress response is triggered.

HASSLES OF LIFE

Most stressors are not momentous or critical; rather they consist of irritating, frustrating, distressing, unexpected or difficult incidents—the hassles of daily life.

Psychologist Richard Lazarus studied the affects of these everyday hassles and found that they had a direct influence on health and well-being. His research also found that "uplifts"— pleasant, happy, satisfying experiences—can balance the hassles of life, and may perhaps also serve as insulators or buffers against the negative effects of hassles.

In his study, Lazarus found a few commonalities in diaries that his subjects kept of each day's hassles and uplifts. Following are his lists of the most frequently named hassles and uplifts among the middle-aged men and women in his year-long study:

HASSLES	UPLIFTS
1. Concern about weight	1. Relating well with spouse or lover
2. Health of family	2. Relating well with friends
3. Rising prices	3. Completing a task
4. Home maintenance	4. Feeling healthy
5. Too many things to do	5. Getting enough sleep
6. Misplacing things	6. Eating out
7. Yard work	7. Meeting responsibilities
8. Property, investment, taxes	8. Visiting, phoning or writing someone
9. Crime	9. Spending time with family
10. Physical appearance	10. Pleasing home environment

If you think about the pressure you are under, you will probably sense that your daily hassles weigh more heavily than episodic life changes.

Hassles, worries, frustrations and obstacles contribute significantly to our overall stress level. Some of them are, of course, beyond our control. Others stem from the way we see things and where we focus our attention. As we will see later, these are aspects of our stress level that we can modify.

EXERCISE 5

Think back over the past month about the regular hassles in your life—things that frustrated, pressured and irritated you at work and at home. These can include the things you thought about as well as actual situations—*anything* that hassled you.

- Make a list of the regular hassles in your life.
- Rank the hassles, from the most severe and disruptive to the least frustrating.
- Look again at each of the hassles in your life. Write down some things you could do to respond more effectively or take better care of the situations.

Think about the uplifts you have experienced over the past month—the pleasant, revitalizing, satisfying events, thoughts and situations.

- Make a list of the uplifts you recall.
- Rank this list, with the most pleasant uplifts first.
- Think of how you might arrange your life to have more uplifts, which might become an antidote to some of your frustrations and stressful hassles.

EXPLORING YOUR REACTION TO STRESSORS

The most important thing to learn about the stressors in our lives—whether they are daily hassles or major life changes—is the way that we respond to them. Your responses are largely under your control and you can make them more or less effective. In this section, you will look at stressful situations from the vantage point of your responses to them.

You need to be aware of the stages of your response. First, is the often neglected period just prior to the stressful situation.

- Could the situation have been foreseen?
- If I had foreseen it, might I have planned an effective response?
- How do I relate to situations when they come up?
- How does my body respond, what do I say to myself, what do I feel and, finally, what do I do?

Responses are not unchangeable. Starting in childhood, we have learned and developed certain habitual styles of response to various situations. These habits often become dysfunctional, especially by the time we are faced with adult realities and responsibilities. We need to change some basic habitual ways of dealing with stressful situations when we find that these habits tend to do us in, rather than support us.

Each time you face a stressful incident, take a moment to look at yourself and examine your responses. Ask yourself:

- What was the trigger?
- What did I think and feel?
- How did I respond?
- How did others around me respond to my response?
- How effective was my interaction?
- What were the incident's negative effects on me?

Asking these questions will make you sensitive to yourself in a new way, which will help you to see how many different stages and possibilities are contained in a single situation.

One of the author's major goals is to help you move from a perception that stress is something that happens to you—you are its victim—to the belief that your reaction to stress is alterable and involves your own reaction to the world around you. To help you do this, you need to keep a daily log of stressful situations for at least one or two weeks.

In this section you will compile a Personal Stress Log to help you look at the regular situations that cause you stress and your response to them. From this log you can discover your response habits.

Begin Exercise 6, your Personal Stress Log, by noting and exploring each event. Patterns in your perceptions and responses will begin to emerge. These are helpful in planning ways to change your response.

EXERCISE 6: PERSONAL STRESS LOG

Carry the log with you during the day. After any incident that leaves you feeling upset, distressed, angry, pressured, aroused, anxious or frustrated, fill out one row of the log. After a few days you will have an ongoing record of stressful incidents in your life and your responses to them.

In each column indicate the following for each incident:

- The date, day of the week and time.
- A few words about the nature of the event, so that you can remember it when you go over the log later.
- Your estimate of how distressing the incident was, on a scale of 1 to 10, with 1 indicating a mild distress and 10 a severe upset.
- A few words about what you did, your own response and activity in the situation—before, during and directly after it.
- Your thoughts and feelings, the things that you said to yourself and felt during and after the incident.
- How the incident left you feeling, physically and emotionally; its cost to you.

Your Stress Response Profile

Reread your logs and records. Review Exercise 6. Summarize your style of responding to stress according to these guidelines:

Frequency: How many times in a day do you encounter distress?

Severity: How severe is the buildup of stress? How distressing are the worst incidents?

Anticipation: Do you expect the incidents to develop, or are they unexpected? Are they isolated or ongoing? If they are unexpected, can you learn how to see potential stressful events before they happen?

Sense of control: How many of the events that distress you can be controlled or changed by you, and how many cannot? Look at the most stressful situations and think about how you might create more control over them. How might you plan to cope with events that you cannot influence?

Engaging or avoiding: Is your tendency to respond to situations by actively doing something about them, or to avoid the situation altogether?

Types of problem situations: What kinds of problem situations cause you distress? Where do you tend to encounter them?

Problem responses: What are the things you do in stressful situations that create difficulty for you?

Desired changes: What is the thing that you would most like to change about your response to stressful situations?

Think about these questions and write down your reflections. This will help you to become familiar with your usual coping responses and begin to brainstorm ways to modify them.

The degree of pressure you feel is your estimate of how much a stressful situation affects you. The higher your score, the more important it is that you do something about

PERSONAL STRESS LOG

Day/Time	Event	Distress Level (1 – 10)	What You Did	What You Thought/Felt	Your Physical Response

a situation. For many minor pressures, putting them aside may be the best strategy. Major pressures usually cannot be avoided and must be resolved directly.

Many unexpected pressures and situations can be anticipated. Like any situation, good or bad, the more we anticipate and plan for it, the more easily we can cope with it or enjoy it. Unexpected situations demand more from us because our bodies and our expectations are not prepared.

Some stressors are unavoidable, like noise levels on the street, while others can be avoided or changed. When we are in a situation that we cannot change or influence, all we can do is take care of our bodies and try to bring ourselves back to baseline levels of rest. Many of us spend too much time trying to change things that cannot be changed, instead of doing something about those situations that can be modified.

When something can be done in a situation, we need to take direct action. Failure to take action is a primary factor in creating stress-management problems. On reflection, in many of the situations that we initially define as being difficult or impossible to manage, we may actually have considerable influence. We need to look closely at our perceptions of personal power and our ability to control, manage and influence the events around us.

EXPLORING YOUR PERFORMANCE UNDER PRESSURE

When our stress levels become too high over prolonged time, we experience what Hans Selye labeled the exhaustion stage of the stress response. Exhaustion demands time off for recovery, and some of us never fully recover our previous energy levels. It makes sense, therefore, to build in rest breaks when we know we are going through a heavy workload.

We also should monitor our body's physiological response during a stress-inducing situation. In this way we can try to regulate our stress level before it becomes a problem. One way to increase self-awareness is to pose a series of questions.

Ask yourself:

- How stressful is this situation going to be?
- How much stress am I experiencing right now?
- What's happening to my breathing right now? How is my behavior being affected right now?

Whatever your combination of sensations, you will be impressed with how dramatically different your respiration is, compared with when you are relaxed.

In a high-stress situation the next questions to ask are:

- What can I do right now to respond to the situation? What can I do to change my body's response?
- What can I do to accept the situation? How can I change my attitude about it? Can I somehow redefine the situation so that it takes on a different meaning for me?

Unfortunately, most situations are not easily changed or even within our sphere of influence. Therefore, changing your response to a situation is frequently the only approach you can take.

- Since I can't change the situation, what value is there in getting excited or tense? Realistically, what is the proper level of stress for this situation?

If you exceed the *proper level*, you waste valuable energy, and you set yourself up to become fatigued, emotionally upset, physically depleted or ill.

- Is this the best way to treat myself right now?
- What are the consequences of allowing myself to get so stressed?

After you have decided that action is required, focus on your breathing patterns. At first, just observe them. Don't make any effort to change them. This simple shift of awareness will have an almost immediate effect.

Now, begin consciously to regulate your breathing. Allow your abdomen to relax. Imagine how your diaphragm is pushing down on your viscera; as your abdominal muscles relax, your abdomen extends slightly.

Begin to breathe slowly in a consciously regulated pattern. There's no need to stop focusing on the situation you are confronting; merely add another layer of awareness to your participation in this situation by watching your body.

THE COSTS OF CHANGE

The stressors that have been most widely studied are life crises and changes. Researchers Thomas Holmes and Richard Rahe were struck by how the presence of many life changes are often followed by serious and minor illnesses. People who experience several changes—negative *or* positive—in the course of the year have a greater risk of becoming ill. For example, college football players who had the most changes in the year preceding the football season had a disproportionately high share of injuries.

Has your past year been stable and consistent or has it had many major or minor changes? If you have had many changes, you are not alone.

What should you do if your life is full of changes? Change does not automatically result in illness. Rather, many changes lower your resistance and you therefore have to take special care of your body. Anticipating future illness and trying to protect yourself is a cornerstone of self-care.

CHANGE AND ADJUSTMENT

Many people who have several life changes begin to fear for their health. They come to the erroneous conclusion that change in itself is harmful to their health, like tobacco. Indeed, as we struggle to adjust, changes and daily demands create pressures, both on our bodies and our psyches. However, research on coping with stress affirms that what matters is not how many pressures and changes we experience, but how we look at them, relate to them and manage their effects.

The purpose of measuring the degree of outside pressure—stressors—in our lives is to begin the process of sensitizing us to the effects of demands upon us. The goal is awareness. For many of us, change and pressure are also sources of challenge, novelty, excitement and creative involvement.

A life without change and demands would not allow us to utilize our creativity, our natural life energy; such a life would be boring and unstimulating. However, increasing our awareness of stressors allows us to think about the effectiveness of our coping. For example, once we realize that change creates pressure, we can anticipate future changes and manage the situation effectively. Or, we can begin to think of ways to deal with chronic daily frustration, hassles and demands.

The Experience of Loss

One type of change is particularly stressful and difficult: the experience of loss. Of course, the loss of someone you love is a devastating and painful experience. But there are other kinds of losses as well. There is the loss of a job, a possible promotion, the loss of a friend or colleague who moves away, or there is the loss of something valuable, perhaps through theft.

Any loss leaves a vacuum in your life. A space and time that was pleasantly filled is now empty. It is reasonable to feel pain and sad feelings, which may last a year or more for the loss of a loved one. After a loss, we need to go through a process of grieving, in which we let go of the person (or thing) that was lost. It is a process of remembering and saying good-bye. Curiously, there is a clear grieving process associated with loss of work or opportunity, which is often complicated by anger, personal shame, feelings of inadequacy and self-blame. Be aware that such feelings are natural and necessary when overcoming a loss.

THINKING: THE HUMAN WAY OF CREATING

Our minds can increase or decrease the amount of pressure that an incident produces within us. During childhood, we develop expectations and beliefs about other people, our self-worth, abilities and the nature of things. All of these affect what we perceive as stressful, difficult or manageable.

Suppose two employees are given a task that is beyond their ability or training. One might mention that and ask for help. She would not see the assignment as particularly overwhelming, so the incident wouldn't trigger a psychophysical stress response. The other person might assume that he was expected to know how to do it and that if he didn't accomplish it, his job would be on the line. He might also assume that asking for help is an indicator of failure. This set of expectations would make the assignment of that task the trigger for an intense stress response. The pressure of these perhaps unwarranted assumptions adds to the difficulty. The stress lies more in the expectations and the meaning the person adds to the task than in the difficulty of the task itself. This is the case with most of the incidents and situations that people find stressful.

Our definitions of situations as well as our expectations and beliefs color all of our experiences of stress. The following list consists of situations that are not necessarily stressful.

- We may have to face a co-worker with whom we have had difficulty in the past.
- A new task may upset our expectations for a peaceful day.
- We may feel that a glance or remark means something about our role or status. In each case it is our mind that is creating the stress, not the situation.

The way we evaluate a situation, its importance and our sense of our capacity to face it determine our response. We may:

- Avoid or give up on a task that we feel is beyond our ability
- Create stress for ourselves due to our self-criticism and annoyance at not having done it.

- Create a fight with someone because we evaluate a situation or remark as ominous or threatening.
- See all situations as invitations for competition, or see everyone else's activities as letting us down.

Managing stress involves exploring the ways that we talk to ourselves, what we assume, the way we define situations and our own evaluation of experiences. The environment creates demands, challenges, changes and pressures. Since stress is a product of our interaction with our world, we can change the amount of stress we are under by changing our perception and response to things.

Our thinking can also lead to burnout by creating self-fulfilling prophecies. For example, a person who does not expect other people to help him may act distant, or may even tell himself that it doesn't pay to try. He may never find out that support is available, because he assumes it is not. We make many assumptions about other people and about ourselves through learned expectations from our personal history, family, teachers and our work life. Often we become so tied to certain types of expectations that we make them come true. Modifying negative beliefs and expectations about ourselves, our ability and situations in the world is central to developing a sense of personal power.

So we see that before a situation can trigger the physiological stress response in a body, it must be filtered through our habitual ways of thinking about the world. Our psyche can decide that a minor daily hassle demands the total physical mobilization of the stress response. Or it can decide to handle a difficult task with no sweat, and therefore not activate the stress response.

We can think of our beliefs, thoughts and feelings about things as a filtering or evaluating mechanism standing between the environment and the activation of the psychophysiological stress response and/or an active coping response to meet the challenge.

Psychologist Albert Ellis calls this the A-B-C cycle of behavior. Event A, which may or may not have something to do with us, takes place in our environment. There is our response, C, to that event B, which is what we say to ourselves, how we see and define the situation, which in turn determines our response, lies between the two.

We can define everything as our problem and burn ourselves out trying to do everything. Or we can tell ourselves that nothing we do will be good enough, which undermines our feeling about our response enough to make us feel weak and powerless, usually even if we handle the situation effectively.

A EVENT STRESSORS	B PERCEPTUAL FILTERS	C COPING RESPONSE
Pressures	Past experience	Psychophysical
Demands	Expectations	stress response
Changes	Evaluation	Burnout
Challenges	Beliefs	Coping response

Our perception of events, or our appraisal of situations, is a key determinant of our level of burnout or balance. In this section we explore the major types of self-defeating, even self-destructive thought patterns that in themselves push us closer to burnout and keep us from mastering the world. Certain types of thinking place us in an unremitting world of overwhelming, even paralyzing, stress.

For Exercise 7 complete Assessment 3 in the Appendix. Using this tool you will explore negative and critical thoughts about yourself and situations. None of the statements on the scale has a right or wrong answer. Rather, they illuminate the way you feel about yourself and the things you expect from the world. From this scale you will have an idea about how positive or negative the conversations you have with yourself are.

CONVERSATIONS WITH OURSELVES

Most of the day, though we may be silent to people around us, we engage in a continual conversation with ourselves. Within our mind, we listen to chatter about what we are doing. Sometimes we talk to ourselves about something about to happen that we may anticipate.

"I'm going to mess it up."

"These things always turn out badly."

"All the other guys at work are out to show me up."

"My job is on the line with this project."

"I just don't know how to do it."

Another person might have a different type of self-talk:

"I can handle everything."

"Things usually work out for the best."

"The people at work like and respect me."

Negative and positive ways of talking to ourselves have a critical influence on our capacity to respond. The body triggers the stress response not only when something threatening is actually happening, but when we simply *think* about something threatening. So the person who is talking negatively to himself, worrying and thinking about all the bad things that might happen, is physically triggering the stress response within his body—even before he confronts the actual event. If the event has already happened—say, a difficult project— thinking over and over about how badly you may have done also triggers the stress response repeatedly until the body becomes exhausted. The results are headaches, gastric distress, diarrhea and other stress symptoms, not so much due to a threatening *event*, but to the way we think about it over and over again.

There are many ways that we create negative and self-defeating conversations with ourselves.

Some of the more common forms of negative self-talk include:

Shoulds: As we choose not to do some things, or to follow other directions, we create stress by telling ourselves what we ought to be doing. We make demands on ourselves based on standards that are unrealistically high or impossible to fulfill.

Criticism: People may tell themselves they have not done well or have done something incorrectly. They are far more severe on themselves than others are.

Blame: People create stress by blaming themselves for situations that are either beyond their control or are perfectly reasonable.

Negative expectations: People create stress by imagining bad things that could happen, which causes their bodies to react as if they were taking place. Such worries can also create negative responses to actual situations.

Wrong assumptions: If a person links an event with the wrong conclusion, the event or response may take on unreasonable significance. Thus, thinking that people dislike you adds to your stress, and also affects your behavior.

Can'ts: When we are afraid of a challenge or we doubt ourselves, we do not look closely at our motivations. Instead, we say that we cannot do something. This creates stress by placing a defect within ourselves, rather than exploring the perhaps good reasons to have doubts, fears or simply not want to do something.

Errors of Thinking

According to cognitive psychologists, common difficulties such as depression, anxiety and stress arise from illogical conclusions that people draw from the events that affect them. These thinking errors can be corrected through careful observation and practice.

Psychiatrist David Burns has adapted the cognitive therapy method pioneered by Beck and Ellis. He lists the most common distortions of thought.

All-or-nothing thinking: Seeing things in black-or-white categories. Any performance short of perfection is a total failure.

Overgeneralization: Seeing one negative event as a never-ending pattern of defeat.

Mental filter: Picking out a single negative detail and dwelling on it exclusively so your vision of everything becomes darkened.

Disqualifying the positive: Rejecting positive experiences by insisting they "don't count."

Jumping to conclusions: Formulating negative interpretations without sufficient evidence. This may involve misreading other people's minds or predicting negative outcomes for yourself.

Magnification or minimization: Exaggerating the importance of errors or problems, or inappropriately belittling the significance of your own assets.

Emotional reasoning: Assuming that your negative emotions necessarily reflect the way things really are.

"Should" statements: Trying to motivate yourself to improve with "shoulds" and "shouldn'ts," as though you were a delinquent child requiring punishment to accomplish anything.

Labeling: An extreme form of overgeneralization; instead of saying "I made a mistake," the person attaches a negative label, e.g., "I'm a loser."

Personalization: Blaming yourself inappropriately as the cause of a negative event.

Reflect on the things that you say about an event just after something difficult or stressful takes place. Think about the conclusions you draw about the world, and about yourself. Reflect upon how realistic and helpful it is for you to come to such conclusions. Many of the above distortions are simply methods of blaming oneself and making oneself helpless to do anything differently. By becoming aware that difficulties may be due to your thoughts and conclusions, you empower yourself to change these thoughts the next time something difficult happens in your life.

Exploring Your Definition of Stressful Situations

Use the above information to complete Exercise 9. Reflect on the things that you said to yourself before, during and after the events listed on your Personal Stress Log.

- What was your frame of mind?
- Were you angry at yourself?
- Were you expecting the worst?

Some people spend their lives either being sick or expecting to get sick. Others have a set of assumptions about people: they never come through, they don't like me. They see their interactions with co-workers as confirmations of their worst fears.

In any stressful event, we make many assumptions about what is happening, what other people mean, want and feel, what needs to be done and what it means to us. These are not aspects of the situation itself, but rather are part of our reading of it. These assumptions color our perceptions and determine the value we place on things. Look at some of the stressful events listed in your log. Note what you assumed and said to yourself at each stage of the situation. Can you see how your assumptions and thoughts contributed to the event's stressfullness?

Even after a stressful event is over, it continues for us in the form of our thoughts and evaluations of what took place. If we feel that we were deprived of our self-esteem or lost face, for example, we may feel chagrined. Yet the other person may not have the same assessment; and a perceived disadvantage or conflict may exist largely inside ourselves. You will begin to see, as you conduct such reflection for each of the stressful events in your log, how much stress you cause yourself via your thoughts, assumptions and evaluations.

EXERCISE 8 — MENTAL RESPONSES TO STRESSFUL SITUATIONS

List the four most persistent stressful situations that occur in your life:

1. _____

2. _____

3. _____

4. _____

For each situation, list the things you assume, tell yourself and expect:

1. _____

2. _____

3. _____

4. _____

For each of the stressful situations write down some of the things you expect from yourself or criticize yourself for, or negative things that you assume about yourself:

1. _____

2. _____

3. _____

4. _____

For each stressful situation, write down some new things that you might assume about yourself and the situation, things that are more positive. What might you say to yourself the next time?

1. _____

2. _____

3. _____

4. _____

_____

THE INNER CRITIC

Our culture respects and rewards achievement and individual excellence, especially in men. From infancy, we are compared with others and urged to do better. Teachers, parents and peers often have high expectations of us. Many of us grow up feeling pressured, feeling that we have not achieved enough success, or trying to achieve unrealistically high goals.

There are many unintended, negative consequences to the drive to achieve and excel. We may have such high goals that nothing feels like success. We may not allow ourselves to enjoy or rest at any plateau or savor any achievement because we are too busy pushing ourselves for more. Another consequence is a secret feeling of unworthiness, of having failed. We may feel we have failed if we are not number one, or if we do not come up to our parents' expectations or their actual achievements. Yet another negative consequence is the growing feeling that people value us not for who we are, but for what we do. Many people feel estranged from what they have done, or distant from their achievements.

Too often, one grows up with an inner voice that is severely critical or doubting of one's abilities. The inner critic is the voice of parents and teachers, sometimes talking to us in far harsher terms than any of the people in our lives do. The inner critic takes away feeling of success and keeps us under relentless, unyielding pressure.

EXERCISE 9

Think about the way you relate to yourself. Do you have a severe inner critic that expects the impossible and doesn't let you rest?

Write down some of the ways that you continually and unconstructively criticize yourself.

_____

_____

_____

_____

_____

_____

_____

_____

_____

_____

_____

_____

_____

_____

- Now look at the list of was that your critic puts you down. Try to evaluate each criticism objectively. Look at what you have done and how well you perform tasks. Determine if your critic is useful, making suggestions for things you need to improve, or simply adding to your pressure and decreasing your ability to relax and feel good about your life.

Becoming aware of the extent to which your inner critic runs your life is an important part of changing. As you look at how you criticize yourself you can see that your critic is not really you; it is the voice of other people. Perhaps you can begin to counter the negative thinking of your critic. Or you can begin to substitute positive statements, supportive and affirmative evaluations of your work.

POSITIVE THINKING

We can enhance the degree of control that we feel over our lives when we learn to modify some of the ways that we talk to ourselves and think about things. Many of the popular books on psychology, motivation and self-care suggest that many of the difficulties in our lives stem from a lack of self-affirmation.

It is easy to dismiss such positive conversations and changes in our beliefs as evasions of our real problems. Nonetheless, the authors' experience is that people who begin consciously, to modify their inner conversations and assumptions report an almost immediate improvement in their performance. Their energy increases and things seem to go better. It's all in their imagination, cynics say, and the authors hasten to agree. Of course it is, but so was the pressure then, were under to begin with.

We live in a world where it is commonplace to blame others for our shortcomings, where negative messages about our own powers and worth are common. The unintended messages we receive from our parents, our teachers and our employers are that we are not competent or not good. We take these messages into ourselves and repeat them until they become the perceived reality, rendering us powerless, incompetent and incapable of responding to things.

Affirmations

Affirmations are positive, personal statements that modify negative personal beliefs and expectations, and motivate us in new directions. In a mechanistic sense, they are new programs that attempt to change the dysfunctional attitudes and expectations that lead to negative results in our life. An affirmation becomes true if we repeat it often enough—it becomes our internal reality. An affirmation takes effect when our behavior and feelings begin to flow from it.

Affirmations can be more or less effective. For example, just repeating to yourself "I will make a million dollars" is unlikely to be effective. Affirmations are not attempts to apply magic to the external world, nor do they create the impossible (although impossibility is a belief we hold about things); affirmations are rather an attempt to modify patterns of thought and belief that limit and frustrate us.

Before you begin to create a set of affirmations for yourself, examine your negative pattern of thought, beliefs and expectations. You have already discovered many ways that self-talk can create unnecessary limits and keep you from coping successfully with the pressure of your life.

Use these rules to make your affirmations effective:

Place yourself in a receptive state of mind by achieving a state of deep relaxation (as detailed in chapter 6), or simply take a few moments to get your body and psyche ready to receive new information. Before you begin, you need to tell yourself you are ready.

Make you affirmations short, clear, unambiguous and specific. Break down complex desires and changes into small, simple directives.

Phrase affirmations in the present tense. You are creating them as a psychic reality that will exist from the moment you state them to yourself.

Phrase them positively, as what you want to do. Avoid negative words like "stop," "not" or "don't." State what you actually want to think, feel and do.

When you repeat your intentions, try to suspend your doubts. Inhibit the tendency to make a negative or doubting commentary. Do not undercut or undermine your affirmations. If you begin to think negatively, say "no" or "stop" to yourself, and continue the affirmation.

Write down your sets of affirmations and place the list where you will see it repeatedly during the day. You need to keep reminding yourself of them to make them concrete and real for you.

Make affirmations a continuing, ongoing part of your life.

Modifying Negative Thought Patterns

You can change self-defeating or negative patterns by using several common techniques:

Check and modify assumptions. If you feel that your job is on the line, or that people don't really like you, or as you become aware of other self-defeating assumptions that you bring to situations, devise a way to clarify the actual situation. Often checking with other people or simply realizing that your assumptions are unrealistic or extravagant can relieve stress.

Relax and tell yourself the opposite. When you hear yourself saying negative things, worrying or anticipating the worst, you can relax yourself (since the thoughts are probably making you tense) and then begin to imagine more positive situations or say more complimentary things.

Use affirmations. People don't compliment other people or themselves as much as they might. When you find yourself being self-critical, write down a list of positive things about yourself, and things that you would like to happen. Place the list where you can read it often, perhaps on the refrigerator or bathroom mirror. Try to repeat these affirmative messages to yourself several times a day.

EXERCISE 10

Write a short beginning set of affirmations that will modify some of the negative things you think to yourself. Create affirmations concerning some of the important areas of your life. Let your affirmations be expansive and enabling. For example, you might create affirmations such as:

- I am healthy and full of well-being.
- My work is meaningful and exciting to me.
- I deserve to be loved and to have the love I desire in my life.
- It's okay to get what I want.
- I will let myself enjoy receiving from people who care about me.
- I will let go of my anger.
- I can accept my feelings as an important part of myself.
- I can get what I want from other people.
- My work supports my creativity and initiative.

_____

_____

_____

_____

_____

_____

_____

Spend a few moments several times a day slowly repeating your affirmations to yourself. As you repeat them, try to imagine how that affirmation is—or can be—true in your life; you might imagine the affirmation as it comes to be part of your life. Actually see yourself changing. Especially in moments of stress or pressure, affirmations will be useful reminders of your potential for change and your commitment to new ways of being.

Chapter Two

EMPOWERMENT: RESPONDING CREATIVELY TO LIFE'S DEMANDS

To many people, personal power means making other people do what we want them to do and having demands come in a predictable sequence so that we can meet them with our planned and anticipated response. Being in control lasts as long as we can make the outside world submit to our will, and as long as it does not surprise us. If the world doesn't play by our rules, we feel our control slipping away.

Our research shows that personal power actually comes from a sense of confidence that we can meet whatever demands come up creatively and effectively. This means that we know our limits, and limit our expectations, as well as utilizing our skills and strengths. The sense of power that healthy people exhibit is a sense of self-reliance, combined with a knowledge that they have a set of skills that enable them to manage even unpredictable, frustrating or slightly overwhelming events.

Each of us has learned a style of relating to demands that sometimes stands us in good stead, protects our health and ensures our success. At other times, our style adds to our difficulty and causes us trouble and pain.

Demands are not presented to us. We choose the ones to take on, and how we see them. Then we determine the nature of our response, which can resolve or alleviate a demand or make it worse. We can respond defensively, to protect ourselves and our psyche, rather than responding offensively to the demand itself. Overall, we have certain basic approaches to most situations, which make up our personal style—our personality. The way we respond to demands is called "coping," and our way of coping is responsible for our health, our illness, the buildup of negative stress within our bodies and psyches, and the degree of burnout or balance we experience in our lives.

EMPOWERMENT AND CONTROL

Burnout can be seen as a failure of self-regulation. It is neither a necessary nor a predictable effect of certain life crises. Burnout sets in when we do not respond directly to demands, or when we overreact or misplace our reaction to events. It breeds within an environment where the individual feels a sense of helplessness to respond to demands and a sense of hopelessness about the future. "I'm not free, I'm not able to make a difference," a person who is moving toward burnout says to herself. This belief or expectation then becomes true simply because the person acts as if it is true. Despite the lack of positive results, this behavior continues over time.

At the opposite extreme is a person who feels empowered to make a difference in her actions. Her power is neither absolute nor infallible. The world still has the power to defeat, frustrate or deprive her of what she wants, but the person who feels a sense of power always knows she has the capacity to choose a meaningful response to any demand. Her choices are not arbitrary, but arise out of a sense of her needs, values and goals; they support her sense of self and respect the realities and regularities of this life. This response can also be creative, playful and novel, not limited by past precedents. The person is not a victim of life, but rather has the capacity to respond creatively and effectively to demands.

The capacity for creative responses is what differentiates the person from the robot or the computer. We can learn, adapt, grow and to a degree, let go of the past. The exploration of the basis of our sense of personal power and its elements keeps telling us that no matter what demands are placed upon us, we can come up with a creative response. Creative responses begin within the individual, in the way he or she organizes reality and reads situations. Human beings are unique in their capacity to anticipate and plan—to create their future—to explore alternatives within themselves and to evaluate the results and make changes, even in mid-action.

The following questions can be approached by studying the pressures and demands that fall upon us, and by looking at the way we organize our inner worlds and the way we visualize ourselves and our abilities.

- What does a person see?
- Does he see opportunities or only missed chances?
- How well does a person acknowledge his own capacities and skills?
- Does she maximize or minimize them?
- In what ways does a person distort situations or read them clearly?

MEANINGFUL CONTROL

People who are able to handle the stress of their lives feel in control of their world. That does not mean that they have total control over everything or everyone around them. In fact, studies of those rare individuals who had total control showed that they were anxious and fearful—but that they felt they could do something about the things that distressed them. When faced with a stressful situation, they pick the aspect of the situation that they can do something about. We use the term *optimal control:* people who manage stress well seem to be in control of their immediate environment.

Some people feel that they cannot control anything; they are victims of their environment and circumstances. These people suffer from undercontrol, or what has been termed the "helpless/hopeless syndrome." These people are depressed and suffer from a variety of stress-related health and emotional problems.

At the opposite extreme are people with "Type A behavior syndrome." These people suffer from overcontrol and take on every project and have to do everything themselves. They find it hard to trust people, who always let them down. Overcontrol, too, is associated with health and stress-related difficulties.

One of the primary qualities of effective stress management is the sense of control we have over our world. We have this

This diagram illustrates the three possibilities.

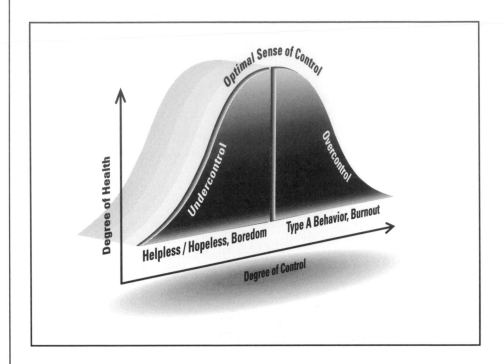

sense of control when we know how to choose situations we can do something about and thereby regularly accomplish clearcut goals and experience success and relaxation. Neither the helpless/hopeless person nor the Type A person can ever experience success or a sense of accomplishment. People at both extremes are never at rest or comfortable. Which type are you?

- How do you approach life?
- Do you tend to see yourself as a victim or as a martyr?
- Do you recognize your limits and respect them?
- Do you select goals and projects, or do you take on everything that comes your way, as if you have to?
- What can you do to bring yourself to the optimal balance point?

ASSESSING AND MODIFYING YOUR COPING STYLE

Our response to each day's demands, crises and challenges depends on the situation, as well as on our personal bag of tricks. We have developed certain preferred, comfortable ways to manage difficulty, to approach tasks and to respond to crises. These are our coping strategies, and they work for us. Some of us have only a few of them and respond the same rigid way no matter what the situation. Others have many responses and fit them flexibly to the task. The self-assessment exercises in this section will help you continue to explore the different ways that you respond to stressful situations.

In Chapter 2 you kept a Personal Stress Log. If you go back and review the log, you will probably recognize recurring patterns and chronic problem areas.

Your coping style is not all positive or all negative. It contains many elements, some of which are helpful in certain situations, and others that might be needed in different circumstances.

For Exercise 11, complete Assessments 4 and 5 in the Appendix. Your responses will create a list of your positive and negative coping responses, and identify what causes the most difficulty for you.

PROFILES OF COPING STYLES

Self-assessment coping styles refer to several ways that people commonly cope with stressful events. The six styles described are coping difficulties—styles of managing stress that in most situations are more dysfunctional than effective. Refer to your responses to Assessments 4 and 5 as you read these descriptions of each dysfunctional style and some ways to make changes.

1. Withdrawal

Withdrawal is a style of avoiding, fearing or otherwise putting off action that would reduce the pressure. In this style, a person maintains the level of stress he is under by not doing something about it. He may be afraid to do what is needed, or he may have all sorts of reasons and rationalizations for what he is not doing. The fact remains that the source of pressure does not go away.

There are all sorts of psychological theories about why people engage in this seemingly dysfunctional pattern. They may be afraid to succeed or they may lack self-confidence. They may have simply gotten into the habit of not acting, or they may not be able to imagine how good it would feel to get things done. They may fear change and risk and wish for things to remain the way they were in the past. The reasons are less important than learning a way to motivate oneself to action.

If you scored high on withdrawal, you are not taking risks, allowing yourself to make changes, completing important tasks and meeting responsibilities. This, in turn, leads to worry, frustration, fear and depression. There are several ways to begin to change.

Make a list of important tasks, personal priorities and major demands on you. List all the good personal reasons that you have for not doing them. You will probably find that you have many fears, emotional complications and other difficulties that prevent you from tackling tasks. Think of some ways to change your reasons for not doing the task. Set a deadline for yourself and try to face the task directly.

Take some time and get yourself into a state of quiet relaxation. Slowly, imagine yourself doing the task. Imagine it in as minute detail as you can. Let your body feel what doing the task is like. Imagine that you are doing the task well and feeling good about it. When you see yourself completing the task, imagine how good you will feel, and the rewards and benefits you will receive from others. Do this exercise several times, over several days.

Create rewards for yourself. At each step of a complicated task—and when you are finished—give yourself a special reward that feels good to you. Also, be alert to the responses of others to your activity as another sort of reward—a boost in your self-esteem.

Think about the little things that you want, or would like to do. Imagine asking someone for a date, trying something new, exposing your feelings or asserting your rights. Each day try to take a risk or two. Watch your own response and how others respond to your initiative.

If you find it difficult to begin, ask yourself why. It may help to imagine what you are afraid of, or to imagine the worst thing that can happen. Then, think about whether you really couldn't accept and live with that worst possible outcome. Imagine the best possible outcome. If you continue to feel a deep inner resistance, the task is probably something that you simply shouldn't do; tell the person who expects it of you that you will not complete the task and some of the reasons why. Some assignments and obligations do not have to be carried out, and your resistance is telling you this.

2. Helplessness

Helplessness is not a fact; it is a way of experiencing oneself. It is the sense that you cannot do things, or that what you can do won't make a difference. Helplessness is usually paired with hopelessness, and this whole style is an extreme form of withdrawal. When demands or needs are experienced, the person freezes and hides. As a consequence, the person never experiences any sense of personal power or ability. The feeling is amplified over time until depression sets in. He experiences himself as helpless, as a victim. The person does not even try to resist or overcome a source of stress, and it seems that the body, like the psyche, gives up and illness begins to take root.

Helplessness is a self-defeating cycle: if you perceive yourself as not having ability, you don't improve or achieve success, which justifies the perception and brings the process full-circle. For this reason, helpful approaches to the problem of helplessness—extreme withdrawal—aim at short-circuiting this self-defeating pattern.

The feeling, of helplessness can be redefined as problem stemming from negative self-talk. Modifying helplessness begins by observing and writing down some of the negative things that you tell yourself about your ability, about the world and about yourself. These self-statements serve to justify continued helplessness.

Look at your list. Try to remove yourself and think about each statement objectively. Is it actually true from your experience, or were there perhaps only one or two events that led to your conclusion? Do something to test your assumption. For example, if you feel that nobody really cares about you and that is why you don't approach anyone or go out socially, you might call up some acquaintances and have a dinner party.

Another area to explore is the expectations and myths you have about your performance. Many people can't begin because they expect unachievable perfection from themselves, or they are frustrated because they are unable to complete tasks. Exploring the nature of your expectations and demands on yourself can lead you to revise them, which in turn frees you for action.

Another approach is to take direct action. People who feel chronic helplessness often say they don't want to do anything until they feel better. However, doing nothing does not make them feel better; it makes them feel worse. Therefore, to reverse the cycle do *anything,* and see how you feel afterward. If you begin to do little things, despite your negative feelings, you'll begin to perk up and experience rewards from what you do. This, in turn, leads to more activity, and the spiral is reversed to a positive direction.

3. Internalizing

If you fill a balloon with air, it eventually bursts. Similarly, when a person tries to hold in more and more feelings, handle intolerable amounts of pressure and do things on one's own, the pressure mounts up. Frustration, resentment and psychophysiological arousal build up. One never gets an opportunity to relax and go back to baseline, to release the stress. One is left after each accomplishment with a residue of unrelieved stress, which takes root in the form of any of the stress symptoms listed earlier.

The following characteristics describe internalizers.

- They keep things to themselves.
- They feel that telling others how they feel is beside the point, sometimes even downright dangerous.
- They fear conflict, or rationalize that sharing feelings is unproductive.
- They keep their pressure to themselves and rarely ask for help.

• They may be seen as paragons of calmness and poise.

Unfortunately, internalizers are often asked to do more and more, because of their nature, and another sort of self-defeating spiral is generated.

Internalizing is common because the model of behavior in our culture includes keeping cool under pressure and not sharing feelings. But there are definite health consequences and costs to internalizing, just as there are self-defeating long-term consequences of the Type A style, which our culture also values. While internalizing is useful in some crisis situations, it is isolating and creates undue tension and unreleased stress.

Most internalizers have the experience of suddenly becoming aware of an almost intolerable buildup of frustration, anger or stress symptoms, such as a headache. They have not been paying attention to their body; all of their attention was trained on their environment, their outer world.

You can change this tendency by practicing the body awareness exercises outlined in Chapter 5. Check in with yourself as you are working and as you begin to experience stress. Note what feelings are building up, how you feel about things. Sometimes just being aware of your feelings, without necessarily expressing them to other people, is enough to help you take steps to change the situation.

Another pathway is to explore your reasons for holding your feelings in. Think of some situations where you did not tell co-workers or family members what you were feeling. It is interesting to note that people who hold feelings in usually hold in both positive and negative feelings. Write down some of your reasons for not sharing feelings. These may be fears of how people will react, anticipation of rejection, resistance or anger from others. They may stem from assumptions about yourself: a strong person does not talk about feelings, he keeps such things to himself. When you explore your reasons, you may find they are less persuasive than you expected.

Separate expression of feelings from demands. Many people feel that when they express a feeling, it is a demand for something from another person. If you express anger, for example, the person you express it to has obligation to do something about it. That is one reason people fear other people's feelings and hold in their own: they fear or recoil from obligations. You can begin to express how you feel without having an expectation that the recipient ought to change as a result of it. Your feeling is important information about you that needs to be stated so that the people around you can know how you are reacting. Many fears and worries are created by speculating about other people's feelings. By gently letting people know how you feel, you will begin to see how many of your fears and negative expectations were groundless.

4. Emotional Outbursts

Emotional outbursts are really the long-term outcome of internalizing, just as helplessness is the long-term outcome of withdrawal. When you hold feelings in, they build up. One way to discharge feelings is to blow up, usually on a safer occasion than the situation where the feeling originally arose. For example, we are concerned about our own performance and instead get angry and make unfair demands on our employees. Or, we are frustrated with our marital relationship and find ourselves blowing up at our children, rather than looking at the actual source of our feelings.

There are two primary purposes of emotional outbursts.

- They release tension in a safe environment.
- They often involve shifting blame and responsibility.

When we are frustrated or under stress, one self-defeating emotional response is to relieve ourselves of responsibility by blaming another person. This process often leads to the curious outcome of two people arguing about who is responsible for something, while neither person does anything about the situation. Shifting the blame is one mode of avoidance of responsibility. The negative consequence of blowing up at or blaming another person is to shift one's own stress and frustration to that person. Blowing up is like tossing a hot potato—the tension is passed along to another person. But the source of the frustration is untouched.

Dealing with emotional blowouts is paradoxically similar to modifying internalizing. It includes becoming aware of emotions when they are being created, and discharging them in the appropriate situation. The person who finds herself blowing up needs to inquire into the origin of these frustrating feelings and find another way to express them. Instead of shifting responsibility for feelings to another person, the process of exploring feelings involves asking yourself why you feel that way. Then you can make changes in the situation that created the feeling, not make demands on or shift tension to other people.

5. Overcontrolling

Keeping things under control is one of the most important and successful methods of stress management. However, the difficulties many people, including those with Type A behavior, experience in coping with stress stem from trying to anticipate every reaction of other people, trying to control every situation and trying to plan for every eventuality. At some arbitrary point, keeping meaningful control over one's environment becomes trying to keep too much under one's control. This creates anxiety because it is impossible. Overcontrolling makes the world more stressful.

We try to keep things under control by accomplishing every task, meeting every obligation and taking care of everything around us. Nothing can be put off or declined. This is tiring and frustrating, in many ways similar to Type A behavior.

Modifying a coping style that tends toward overcontrolling involves several elements. First, priorities and tasks need to be evaluated, and tasks that can be dropped, or for which help can be discovered, are modified.

Second, moving away from too much controlling involves confronting the fear of not being in control. Take a moment to ask yourself the following questions.

- Why do I do all these things in my life?
- Am I afraid to displease people around me, or disappoint them?
- Am I afraid of failure?
- Do I doubt my worth, or feel that I am unappreciated?

If you have feelings like these, you are not likely to feel better simply by doing everything that is humanly possible. There will always be reason to fear others' opinion or your own abilities. Looking honestly at the feelings and attitudes that lie behind your behavior is the most effective way to make changes in dysfunctional coping strategies.

Type A Behavior

The most clearly established connection between a response to stress and health is the connection between Type A behavior and all forms of coronary heart disease. Along with proper diet, regular exercise and not smoking, the modification of this method of coping is one of the most important ways that a person can prevent illness, as well as prevent all sorts of minor stress symptoms.

Type A behavior, as defined by cardiologists Meyer Friedman and Ray Rosenman, and psychologists David Glass and C. D. Jenkins, is a blend of emotional responses and activity in response to the demands of life, especially in relation to work tasks. According to Rosenman and Friedman, Type A behavior is:

> *An action-emotion complex . . . [that] can be observed in any person who is aggressively involved in a chronic, incessant struggle to achieve more and more in less and less time, and, if required, to do so against the opposing efforts of other things or persons.*
>
> *This chronic and incessant struggle . . . together with a free-floating, but covert, and usually well-rationalized hostility make up the Type A Behavior pattern. The sense of urgency and hostility give rise to irritation, impatience, aggravation and anger.*

Friedman notes that Type A behavior may initially bring about career success and achievement and some life satisfaction. But the negative consequences soon outweigh the gains. The Type A person has difficulty in working with others and in adjusting to change and the unexpected. The frustration builds as the person never achieves satisfaction or peace. In addition, over time the Type A person becomes more and more one-dimensional, as he or she gives up hobbies and leisure activities, and even limits involvement with family and friends. Often a traumatic event—breakup of a marriage, loss of a job, being passed over for a promotion, failure of an effort—can lead to a reevaluation of this style of coping.

The Type A behavior pattern is extremely common—and indeed encouraged—within our culture. It can also be modified. People can learn new ways to cope, and once they find these methods rewarding, and develop new habits, they are much more effective at coping with the stress of their lives.

Friedman's change program involves four components:

1. Reevaluate every one of your activities to trim their activity level way down. Learn time management and prioritizing.

2. Recognize your hidden anger and hostility, rather than denying it. Learn new ways to handle anger openly.

3. Practice and drill daily in walking, eating, talking and driving at a slower pace.

4. Pay attention to the here and now, and react posititively, even with pleasure, to situations that before would be frustrating.

COPING AND CONTROL

The healthiest and most effective people have learned to achieve a balance between taking care of themselves—self-renewal—and taking on the challenges that are presented to them. These people optimize their sense of personal control, seek challenge and are involved in their work. They select the challenges they will face or those they set as their personal goals, and they face them with a minimum of avoidance and evasion. However, they do not neglect the needs of their bodies or push themselves too far, and they do not always go it alone. They call on help and supportive resources from other people.

People have problems in coping when their responses to stressful situations do not get the desired result. They either overrespond, underrespond or respond in the wrong place or direction.

When we respond to situations automatically without reflection or planning, using habits learned years before, we rob ourselves of flexibility.

Action vs. Self-Support

When we face a stressful situation, our efforts to cope can take two basic directions. We can respond directly to the situation itself, by doing something to diminish the pressure, but coping usually involves more than that. In the stress response, our body becomes aroused physiologically, and we also have a strong emotional response. Whether we pay attention to them or not, stressful events arouse fears and angers. Our self-esteem or our well-being is threatened, and we often need to minister to an injured psyche. Thus, coping consists of handling a situation and also protecting and regenerating ourselves.

This double task is where the difficulties most often arise. Sometimes we cope with stress exclusively by handling the situation itself, without much attention to our emotional or psychological needs. Other coping responses focus primarily on self-protection, the preservation of our self-esteem, and do little to modify the external situation. Effective coping demands attention to both types of need.

When we look at the six dysfuncional coping styles again, begin to notice that the dysfunctional aspects of these reponses lie in the way that they tend to protect the psyche more than they manage the demand.

Withdrawal and Helplessness

Looking more closely, we see that withdrawal and helplessness are motivated by a feeling that we are not up to meeting the demand or accomplishing the task. Since we doubt ourselves, we pull back from the challenge. Naturally, the outcome supports our negative opinion of ourselves, since we do not change the situation that faces us. We then continue to feel bad about ourselves, and the pressure or demand continues to loom over us.

Internalizing and Emotional Outbursts

These dysfunctional responses get us into trouble because they are poor attempts to deal with the emotions produced by stressful situations. The internalizer misses the chance to get help and emotional support from others. Many internalizers do not feel that other people care about them or their problems, and so they hold back. The person who has emotional outbursts experiences a variation of this same problem. He internalizes distress over a period of time until the pressure leads to an explosion. When it comes, it is out of proportion to the trigger event, and more often than not acts to push other people away, people who might otherwise be helpful resources. People are bewildered by the emotional intensity, or they feel attacked.

For example, one manager continually berated his employees, thinking that the work had to get done. But he never explored the possible effects of his angry outbursts on the behavior of his employees. The unintended consequence was that his staff began to withhold information and avoid him, diminishing everyone's effectiveness.

Overcontrolling and Type A Behavior

These two patterns have some similarities. Overcontrolling is rarely effective, because other people respond by resisting attempts to be controlled. The Type A behavior pattern joins overcontrol with overscheduling and an inability to tolerate frustration. Both responses may handle some demands effectively, but over time they lead to exhaustion and burnout.

Active Coping

People who feel they respond successfully to stressful situations have incorporated the three aspects of active coping into their behavior.

Support Seeking: We cannot live in the world alone, and many of the dysfunctional styles of coping—withdrawal, helplessness, iternalizing, emotional outbursts, Type A behavior, overcontrolling—involve moving away from supportive relationships with other people. They involve not sharing feelings and tasks. Support seeking involves creating positive working relationships. It is perhaps the best insulation against the negative effects of stress.

Diversion/Tension Release: Taking care of your body and allowing regular activities to help release the tension that builds up during the day are crucial to effective coping with stress. Sometimes diversion can seem like avoidance but, like control, it is a matter of balance and whether one returns to the work task renewed and refreshed.

Direct Action: Eventually, most tasks cannot be avoided. The more we take action to work on what is needed in our environment, the more we feel in control, and the more tasks we eliminate, the more we diminish the source of our stress.

When you face a stressful situation, ask yourself these questions:

How do I manage or take care of the demand or pressure? Does my response leave the demand or pressure untouched, or do I do something about it? Of course, we cannot simply decide that a demand is not our problem. Many people reduce stress by realizing that many of the tasks they take on are really meant for someone else. But all coping must effectively do *something* about the source of a demand or it will be ineffective and lead to future stress.

How am I taking care of my emotional response to the pressure, and protecting my body and psyche? In evaluating coping styles you need to look at how much of your response is helpful or self-defeating in taking care of your psyche. For example, as a boss you may feel insecure about what is expected of you. In response, you may give your employees the message that you don't like to hear about problems or bad news. Therefore, you are never faced with potentially threatening and ego-deflating information. However, this strategy, like many ineffective coping strategies, loses its effectiveness over time. If you remain defensive, you might switch to scapegoating by blaming other people, rather than dealing with the demand or task itself.

Am I getting what I want, what I need and what I intend from this coping strategy? Many ineffective responses continue, despite evidence that they do not get us what we want or expect. Look also at the unintentional consequences of your coping behavior. For example, taking a drink or smoking when we feel pressure produces clear, long-term negative effects. We may be using up resources to get something managed today that will destroy us tomorrow.

In general, we can look at the dysfunctional methods of coping as attempts to manage situations by either exerting too much or too little control over the environment.

STRESS PERSONALITIES

Each of us has a *stress personality*, a predominant style of coping with stressful situations. At the extremes, some people try to exert too much control over their environment, while others don't exert enough. A person need not be representative of only a single style. Most of us have two and sometimes three predominant styles, which we use for different settings or types of situations. We have, for example, styles of coping at home and at work.

EXERCISE 12

Look at the descriptions of stress personalities that are common to undercontrol and to overcontrol.

- Which personality might be applied to you by the people around you?

_____

_____

_____

- Write down your three most prevalent stress personalities.

_____

_____

_____

_____

Like most aspects of stress management, these personalities are self-defeating or ineffective only when they become extremes, or when a person becomes so inflexible that he she responds the same way to all kinds of stress. Each personality is useful in some situations.

OVERCONTROL PERSONALITIES

Take-Charge Doer: This person takes on every task believing that only he can do it right. He takes over everyone's work and doesn't think of sharing or dividing activities. Consequently, he is continually overloaded and alone.

Competitor: This person sees every task as a competition between herself and other people. She needs to be the best, to outdo others.

Rescuer: This person feels that his mission in life is to help another person or all other people. He is always thinking of service, and of the other, although often he does not ask the others if they want help.

Impatient: This person has a short fuse that life is continually setting off. Frustration is constant, since everything is a source of frustration.

Angry Demander: This person gets things done by angrily demanding help from others, which often results in the other people not doing the task. This type of leader or co-worker is a source of stress for other people, and is usually not effective in getting what she wants.

Conflict Avoider: This is a yes-man who will say or volunteer anything just to make sure that people do not clash. He never states his views and ends up doing things that he doesn't want to do or doesn't think should be done. Everything is held in, as the person tries to satisfy everyone. Although it is never shown, frustration is likely.

UNDERCONTROL PERSONALITIES

Helpless Victim: This person feels that she has no power over the events in her life, and that nobody in the environment is out to support her welfare. She reasons that none of her actions will make a difference, so why should she try? This person exhibits anger, self-pity and is full of reasons why circumstances have made her fail.

Anxious Worrier: This person's life is controlled by fear of past, present and future difficulties. He is afraid of failure, which paralyzes him, causing the worst to happen. His mind is occupied with negatives, fears and self-criticism.

Avoider: This person turns away from responsibilities, tasks and difficulties. This works at times, but eventually the lack of engagement in problem solving leads to disaster. This strategy is not to be confused with a strategy that aims at a balance of rest and activity and respects the body's needs.

Creative Dreamer: This person is full of plans, ideas, projects and an intense feeling of creativity, but is not willing to follow through on them. While the positive, creative thinking may offer some stimulation the lack of activity eventually catches up.

Effective and Ineffective Coping

To conceptualize strategies for coping with stress, imagine two extreme coping styles. On the positive end of the spectrum is the *Active Stress Manager* who does what he or she can to plan, anticipate and respond directly to pressures and demands. At the negative extreme is the *Passive Victim* of stress who avoids effective action and makes the pressure and demands of his or her life into insuperable obstacles. Most people lie somewhere in between.

ACTIVE STRESS MANAGER	PASSIVE STRESS VICTIM
Puts energy into areas that can be managed.	Leaves many things to chance and fate.
Anticipates and plans for the future.	Does not think ahead.
Has a reservoir of time and energy for the unexpected, unplanned and crisis events.	Faces deadlines by cramming at last minute.
Has an accurate perception of both threats and support from the environment.	Demonstrates little foresight or anticipation.
Takes time to evaluate alternate strategies.	Takes on tasks that cannot be completed or are overwhelming.
Adapts a strategy to reduce stress directly.	Does not set clear priorities.
Takes care of self and body.	Lets problems accumulate.
Avoids overloading capacity by pacing and relaxing.	Sees environment as threatening.
Seeks help and support as much as possible.	Has compulsive, stereotyped responses to all threatening, stressful situations.
Manages time by focusing on priorities.	Increases level of stress with his or her reaction.
	Lacks pacing, self-care and diversion.
	Works alone, does not call on resources.

MODIFYING YOUR COPING STRATEGY

With your awareness of your coping style assets and liabilities, and with the information about active coping with stress, you can consider and plan new ways to respond to stressful situations.

EXERCISE 14

Read over the list of your most stressful situations in your Personal Stress Log. Beginning with the most difficult or pressing, ask yourself these questions:

How much control might I have over this situation?
This is a multifaceted question. At first you will be tempted to say that you don't have much control. Yet in our experience everyone underestimates their possible control. For example, you might look at a problem and decide that you can have no effect on it. However, you might gain control when you see that it isn't your problem, and that nobody really expects you to solve it. The sense of freedom comes from increasing control by making the decision that you don't have to handle it. If you come up with other potential ways that you could manage the situation, you will have started to brainstorm about how you might handle it differently.

What are the obstacles to handling this effectively?
There might be a lack of time or resources, or a problem with another person who is also involved in the job. Careful analysis and exploration of the nature of the obstacles to responding to a problem is often illuminating. Think of some of the ways these obstacles might be diminished or neutralized.

How do my personal or emotional responses or sensitivities get in my way?
Here you will look at how habits of managing situations, emotional hurts and prior expectations interfere with change in your ways of responding.

What are alternate ways to manage this situation?
This is the time to draw up a list of all the other ways that you might think about and react to this situation. You might find it hard to think of yourself doing things differently, so maybe you can think instead of how other people you know would handle it. Let yourself brainstorm about alternatives; do not evaluate them or plan anything new.

Remember the guidelines for change at the end of Chapter 1. Don't expect to draw up a plan and just make changes in your response. Rather, you first need to develop a mind-set that accepts your willingness and commitment to making changes.

Imagine Change

This is a method that peak performers such as athletes use.

- Sit in a quiet place and close your eyes.
- In your imagination, go over every step of the reaction to pressure that is ineffective.
- Try to imagine every detail of the event as it occurred in the past.
- Pay attention also to any physical and emotional reactions that you can recall.

Now let yourself imagine the event taking place again, but this time imagine yourself reacting differently. Make it clear to yourself that you do not have to react differently in action, you are merely playing with other ways to react. Try to imagine yourself doing something different as clearly and vividly as your last recall. You will not find it hard to envision how your body will react to the new behavior, and what other consequences will result. In effect, you are trying out new possibilities in the laboratory of your imagination.

Do this imagination exercise again, this time imagining another way you might manage the situation. You will begin to see that you have an almost infinite variety of responses.

Now let yourself reflect on the difficulties and unintended consequences of your typical way of managing this type of situation. Select a new way of responding that seems feasible and achievable by you. Imagine yourself doing this. Reflect on your fears and feelings about actually changing in practice. If you feel ready to try something different, make a commitment to yourself to do what you imagine the next time a similar stress arises.

Risk, Change and Growth

As you begin to make changes in your responses to pressure, you will encounter various types of emotional resistance. You may feel or say things like "I just can't" or "That just isn't me." Or you may experience fear about doing things differently, especially if it means facing situations you have avoided in the past. *All* change efforts encounter fear and resistance. That is why psychologists say that making changes involves risk. Risk involves danger from outside, and includes the danger of hurt to our psyche.

Ironically, to overcome pressure we have to risk the very hurt that our psyche wants to avoid. We need to ask people to do things, and submit our work to others for their evaluation. We may experience rejection, confrontation, conflict and disconfirmation. However, if we do not take the risk, we foreclose the possibility of a successful change. More often than not, our fears are unrealistic and inaccurate.

Achieving greater personal power and coping with pressure involves taking psychological risks. A person can grow and expand only to the degree that he or she moves into new territory. Without risk, there is little chance of growth.

The ultimate stability is death. If a person is to stay alive and resist illness and difficulty, he or she must grow, change, expand and take in new circumstances. Demands and pressures are a part of life, and we need to think about our ways of responding to them. Stress symptoms and burnout are both signs that we are going against our natural human grain and struggling to keep things from changing when the environment and ourselves both resist.

TIME MANAGEMENT

For many people stress takes the concrete form of the clock. Time is the enemy—because there isn't enough of it to get things done. Clearly, however, it is not time but the way that a person relates to it that creates stress. Time management is looking at how you approach and organize tasks to make sure that you accomplish what you want, instead of finding yourself doing what you don't want or need to do.

Everyone has at one time or another pleaded with the powers that be for just a little more time. Since neither scientific nor even psychic powers have yet developed a way to increase the length of an hour or a day, learning to manage the time that you do have is the next best thing. In essence, time management is a combination of how you think about using the time you have and how you actually use your time.

There are two major ways of modifying how you use your time—from the inside and from the outside. How you think about a task has a lot to do with how you approach it. Do you think of how overwhelming this vast project is, or do you break it down into manageable steps and then proceed? The latter is an example of managing from the inside. On the other hand, distractions and pressures from the outside may be the major determinant in your ability to complete a project. If you have too many phone calls or visitors, you can't think clearly and will have trouble getting your work done on schedule.

WORKING IN CHAOS—MODIFYING THE MESS

We've all been in a situation where our environment is too distracting to get anything done—noise from the outside, interruptions, clutter, a general feeling of disorder. Environmental distractions often play a big part in eating up our precious time. Tension is created any time we begin a task that is surrounded by chaos. Juggling too many tasks takes up thinking space that could be used for other work. Making a list of things to be done releases you from the chaos and focuses your attention on the task at hand.

Take a look at your work area. Is it a paper forest, overrun with underbrush and fallen pine needles? Then it's time to create a parking place for all those papers.

• Organize your papers into bunches by project or category.

- Make temporary folders where they can rest until you you need them, out of sight.
- Designate one place for papers that you don't know what to do with.

At the end of the month, go through these papers and throw out anything that you haven't needed in the month. Chances are that you won't need it later and if you do, you can probably get a copy from someone else who has not been such a savvy paper prioritizer.

In your sorting process keep a folder of papers that can be read during odd moments, when you are on hold or in between meetings. This quick-stop file can be useful for things that are not of immediate importance but that do need to come to your attention.

Now that you have created parking places for all your papers, make it a goal that you will handle a paper only once. Pick it up and make a decision about what to do with it. Shuffling papers over and over again leads only to not getting anything done. A well-known time management expert tells how he broke himself of paper shuffling. Whenever he picked up a paper he would tear a one-inch strip off the bottom. As his papers became shorter and shorter he began to understand how much time he was spending passing his papers around. Another modification of this is to put a red dot on the paper each time you handle it. The freckled look will begin to give you an idea of how much time you waste.

THE TIMING OF INTERRUPTIONS

All of us need some continuous thinking time. A recent study of time usage showed that, on the average, people are interrupted every ten minutes! Gaining this important thinking time is often the result of creatively managing the external environment to reduce outside stimulation. Some companies have created strategic, companywide *quiet time* at a certain hour of the day when everyone agrees not to call or otherwise interrupt anyone else. Some have created a flag system for their doors: a red flag means do not disturb, a green flag means it's okay to come in. It's important that there be places where people can get away to have quiet time. Conference rooms and special *think tanks* can be created to allow people to organize their work. One executive found herself in such a chaotic situation within the office that she often went to her car in the parking lot to gain some uninterrupted silence.

Your situation may not be as desperate as hers, but there are certainly times when people dash into your office wanting attention right now. Closing the door minimizes this, but it also gives people the feeling of your unavailability. A useful strategy might be to meet people at their desks. It's often a compliment to them and it enables you to get up and "let them get back to their work" in a friendly manner.

Another powerful interruption is the telephone. Most businesspeople allow the phone to interrupt them at will. Many people have even found that they have a psychological dependency on the telephone, needing to respond to it no matter when and where. In this case the phone is mastering you, not vice versa. What can you do to manage your phone time? The first strategy is not to get on the phone in the first place. Have someone else screen your calls or hold them until you can call back. Some people set up call-back times when they return calls. Use closed-ended questions, ones that can be answered with a yes or no, to keep conversations brief and to the point.

MEETING THE TEST

The need to manage longer and larger conversations occurs in everyday meetings. Since meetings are important arenas of decision making, information sharing and idea generation, it's important to know why you are having the meeting, what items are to be discussed there and what decisions are to be made. Information should be made available beforehand in an agenda so people will be prepared when they arrive.

- Begin meetings on time.
- Lock the door to the meeting room indicating that lateness will not be tolerated.
- Schedule a ten-minute meeting for 2:00 and leave at 2:10, regardless of arriving stragglers.
- Stand up throughout the meeting to decrease the discussion and move people toward faster decisions.
- Make sure a meeting is the appropriate way to handle a matter.

Don't use $100 of staff time to make a decision worth $25. Schedule meetings to end at the beginning of lunch or at 5:00. You'll be surprised how often your sessions end on time. Constantly ask yourself and those present how you can make this meeting more effective next time.

DECIDING TO DECIDE

Indecision and procrastination are two of the biggest wastes of time. Stopping to weigh all the factors involved before coming to a decision often leaves you in the dust and makes your carefully crafted decision out of date.

Think about your decision-making style in terms of a strikeout average. Babe Ruth was the king of home runs as well as of strikeouts. He wasn't afraid to swing at a ball that looked as if it had potential for a hit. This netted him numerous strikeouts, and produced more winners than anyone else. Sticking your neck out in decision making increases the chances of your being right more often.

If you find yourself being indecisive, write down your areas of question and list your reasons for and against the issue. If you are still indecisive, look at your expectations of yourself by asking a few questions.

- How much perfection do you expect from yourself?
- How much excessive effort do you expend to meet this expectation?
- How much is this costing you in time and effort? Your internal standards may be making extra work for you and keeping you from work that would have a higher payoff.

Help yourself focus on items that have potential by asking yourself what's in it for you when you finish the project. Check your motivation to complete it. Unless you receive some sort of recognition, monetary reward or personal feeling of accomplishment, you may find yourself conflicted about finishing the project.

If, after asking yourself these questions, you still find yourself putting off a project, chances are you feel that the project is too large to take on or impossible to finish. What is often paradoxically true about projects of this nature is that they have the highest payoff because of their complexity and their long-term, strategic impact on the business. High payoff items are often vague, difficult to do and do not fit easily into timetables. They need some special approaches to make them manageable.

When undertaking a project that is hard to begin because of its complexity or size, break it into steps or stages. If there aren't any, create them.

- When working on large projects, get a partner who will encourage you toward your goals.
- Meet regularly to form a support team; call each other when you're discouraged.
- Acknowledge the complexity of what you have undertaken and keep your goal in sight.
- Decide on a payoff when you finish the project and reward yourself with it.

When working on a number of different projects at the same time, it's helpful to keep Pareto's principle in mind:

> 20 percent of what you do nets 80 percent of your results.

The most effective use of time is when it is used on projects that will produce the most results. Focus on the results rather than the process. Target the projects that will make the most difference in the long-range objectives of your company or department.

Many people confuse effectiveness with efficiency. Efficiency is doing anything right; effectiveness is doing the right thing right. Don't get caught stomping ants while there are iguanas climbing the walls.

Part Two

SHARING AND CONNECTING

Chapter Three

CREATING SUPPORT SYSTEMS AND NETWORKING

We live within a web, a network of relationships with others—family, co-workers, friends, service professionals and acquaintances. We cannot think of ourselves as separate from our relationships. Our sense of who we are comes out of the care and responses from the people closest to us. What we are capable of doing is similarly dependent on who we have around us and who we know to call upon.

The essential goods and services of human life, both tangible and intangible, derive from the people around us. When we are under pressure, we draw on the experiences and encouragement of friends, and we seek solace and caring from our loved ones. If we lack any of these supportive resources, our test will be that much more difficult, that much more demanding.

Coping with stress depends not only on our inner resources and abilities, but also on the quality, quantity and range of the community of people who inhabit our lives. We live within various social networks, such as the personal relationships from which we receive emotional support, maintain a positive personal identity and obtain resources, information, services and access to more social contacts.

These networks act as social support groups. The process of contacting people you know, to help you get something accomplished, or for help, is what we will call *networking*. In overcoming stress and burnout, the abilities to create supportive relationships and to network are essential.

Think about all the people in your life who in some way give you encouragement. This could be verbal or nonverbal support, or even just the security of knowing that they are on your side. A support system is a resource pool, on which you can draw selectively to support your choice of direction. Through this encouragement, you end up feeling stronger about yourself.

The people around you, especially those closest to you, help to validate your competence and self-worth. They can pitch in when you need to get things done, offer information and resources, help you cope with difficulties and provide willing ears for emotional support and caring. They help you gain new competencies, undertake new challenges and attain objectives.

When you go out on a sunny day, the glare of sunlight on your unprotected eyes creates stress and makes it difficult to see. Many people use sunglasses to filter out the harmful rays. We can think of stressors and stressful life situations in a similar way. If we have to handle them alone, they will be difficult and we may be overwhelmed. But when we have help from other people, we can accomplish tasks and respond to pressure easily, with less pain and damage.

Think about a difficult task or demand—moving to another house, taking a new job in a new city, beginning a major work project. You might become overwhelmed by doing all this alone or even with the help of a supportive friend or spouse. Imagine how it would be if other people in your family and some friends pitched in to help with all the tasks. Imagine that people from the new job meet you and invite you to their house, and help you find your way around the new city.

THE NATURE OF SUPPORT

We use the phrase "social support" to describe a series of relationships with significant people with whom we share common experiences. What makes them different from acquaintances is a sense of connectedness that comes from a shared experience or belief system. These people form a net and provide a *social inoculation* from everyday pressures and crises. In addition, they provide valuable problem-solving information, remind us of who we are aside from this particular stressful situation and give us a sense of belonging where we are valued for ourselves.

It is hard for many people to maintain these long-lasting relationships because of geographic mobility. We often experience disruption in the relationships we have formed and find it difficult to maintain those connections over time. This mobility is embedded in the very values our society holds dear. We emphasize the importance of individual effort and initiative, which has led us to a lifestyle where we have a strong sense of competition and individual responsibility, often keeping us from seeking support of any kind.

Instead we need to learn to create and sustain less permanent relationships. If we move to a new job every few years, we quickly need to discover the people in the company who know how to get things done, and make contact with our direct work group as well as with a broader group of employees so that we can have a sense of the company as a whole and feel at home within it. Similarly, facing the frequency of divorce and temporary intimate relationships, we have to learn to make relationships with people who can care for us, even if that care and support does not last forever.

Finding support, creating relationships and making connections are skills that we need to develop to operate in a world of change. Even though our personal support networks will be in flux, we need to be aware of that, and develop and nurture the relationships that we do have.

MAPPING YOUR SUPPORT NETWORKS

Since your social support is an important factor in surviving everyday stress and strain, it's important to examine what your social support networks look like.

You can think of personal support networks as a series of rings around you, which act as cushions to lessen the effect of whatever stress occurs. A large, varied support network, and a small, tight, intimate network are both helpful. The type of support network and the number of people in your life who are available to you, of course, depend on the type of person you are. Some of us are gregarious, while others are more introverted and may have only a few close friends. However, what seems to be important is not the number of people, but their relationship to you. The breadth of relationships, providing you with multiple layers of cushioning, seems to be an important factor in maintaining health.

This section contains questions to help you map and explore the several types of social support networks.

For Exercise 15 examine the map on page 87 with a series of concentric circles. In the innermost circle is the label "me," because you are at the center of each of your social networks. Each succeeding circle represents a different degree of closeness to you. The rings closest to the center are for the people closest to you. The circles are further subdivided into five wedge-shaped sections, each one representing a different context or environment, or a different network: family/relatives, friends, neighbors/community, co-workers and service/professional resources. There will be, of course, some overlap; a person may relate to you in more than one category.

Starting with the circle closest to you, fill in the names of the people in each of your networks. You might place a neighbor who is also a co-worker in several networks. Place her corresponding to the degree of closeness you feel for her in that context. For example, you may not see that person much at work, but you may see her every day at home.

When you have entered all the names, draw a line between each set of people who know each other. All the people in your family, or in your company, may know each other. Therefore there will be many interconnecting lines. This is your personal network.

The Major Types of Support Networks

Family or intimate network: Traditionally, there was a nuclear family, spouse and children, and the extended family living nearby. Today, many people are not married, and have developed a family-like network of close friends, lovers or old roommates who act like a family.

Friendship and community networks: These are the people in your community and your social life, and may even include some people from work with whom you share social time. These are the people you might call on for help in dealing with various stressful situations—moving, breakup of relationship, etc. These are also the people you see every day. They form both your community environment and, in the case of friends, a continuing

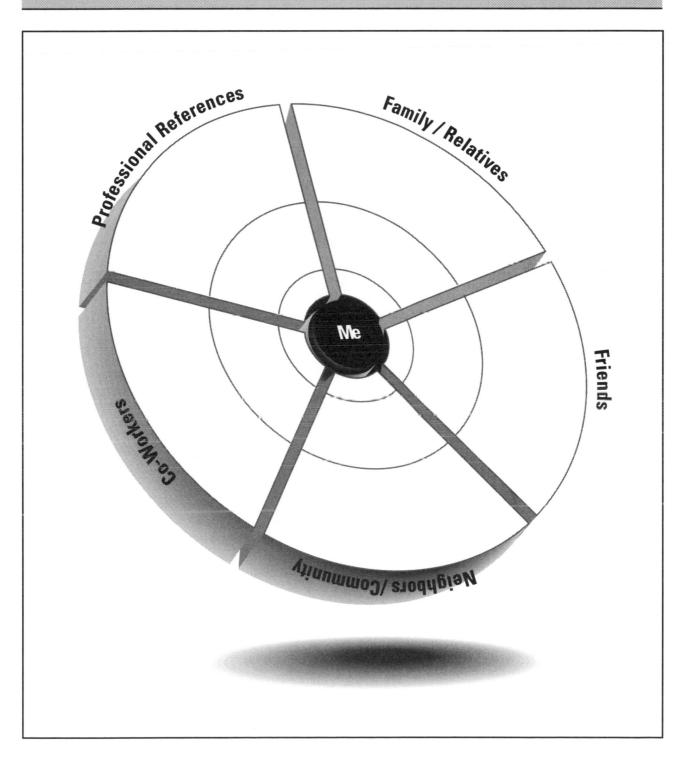

source of support as you move or change. Often your friends are carriers and historians of your personal history and identity.

Work network: These are the people with whom you work and on whom you could feel free to call for work-related support, advice or information. These can be mentors, people who take an interest in your career development, or built-in support resources like employee relations staff or employee assistance counselors.

Service and professional network: This network consists of helpers outside your usual pathways, and includes people like clergy, counselors, home repair people, therapists, consultants and anyone who is a trained helper. One advantage of this network is that you may choose exactly whom you wish to include and make a contractual arrangement with time limits.

Functions of Support Groups

Support networks provide a number of important functions:

Role models: showing you what is possible, what works in certain situations, and alternative approaches

Motivation: reminding you of common interests and goals

Nurturance: friendship and close contact

Help: assistance in times of crisis

Mentoring: respect for your skills and encouragement for new ways to use them

Referral: connection with resources, systems of support and knowledge of how certain procedures work

Challenge: encouragement to take on new responsibilities, make needed changes and stretch yourself beyond your present limits

We get different things from different people in our support groups. There are people to play with, work with, teach us and offer professional advice. (See Exercise 16.)

For each role or function that you might expect from other people, list the one or two most important people to whom you turn. Go back and estimate on a scale of 1 to 5 how helpful, satisfying or supportive your contact with that person actually is (1 = not very effective, 5 = very effective).

You may find that you list the same person or set of people several times; many support people perform several functions. As you go through the list you will begin to see patterns. Circle the areas where you feel that you need, or would like, more support. Which members of your network do you rely on too much, and which members might you rely on more often? Are there areas where you cannot think of a support person who is, or might be, available to you?

The strengths and weaknesses of your support networks will become clear when you complete this profile.

EXERCISE 16 — PERSONAL NETWORK PROFILE

The People I Turn To:	How Helpful Are They? (Scale 1–5)

1. For Close Friendship

_____

_____

2. To Share Problems

_____

_____

3. To Play With

_____

_____

4. For Expert Advice

_____

_____

The People I Turn To:	How Helpful Are They? (Scale 1–5)

5. **To Energize Me**

_____

_____

6. **As Teachers**

_____

_____

7. **As Helpers**

_____

_____

8. **As Mentors**

_____

_____

9. **For Acceptance and Approval**

_____

_____

10. **To Help Me Discover and Try New Things**

_____

_____

11. **For Professional Contacts and Access**

_____

_____

The People I Turn To:	How Helpful Are They? (Scale 1–5)

12. For A Good Time

_____

_____

13. When I Am Hurting

_____

_____

14. When I Need Good Advice with a Problem

_____

_____

15. When I Want to Be with Someone Who Knows Me Well

_____

_____

Support in the Home

It comes as no surprise that your family, or the people who are closest to you and live with you, is the most important support group in protecting you from stress.

To manage stress effectively and maintain balance in your life, one of the best resources is a household that is a safe refuge. In terms of your stress level, living alone may be preferable to living in an embattled household. Also having people around you to whom you can turn to share pressures, fears and struggles is helpful in coping with pressure that cannot be modified. Both friends and family can perform this function.

The support and help from your family, or from the people closest to you in your everyday life, take several forms.

- There is help with tasks and meeting the day's demands—errands, housework, child care and financial support.
- There is also support in having someone to talk to and share things with, for emotional release as well as for helpful suggestions.
- There is the knowledge that somebody accepts you as you are and cares for you.
- And finally, there is the support of having someone to do things with, to share hobbies, leisure activities and have fun.

MOBILIZING YOUR NETWORKS

Think again about your personal networks and the support people in your life. Do you notice some areas in which you would like to increase your resources? Here are some general thoughts about building support.

If people ask themselves why they don't have more friends and support in their work and personal lives, they most often answer that people aren't available. In fact, the major obstacles to building more supportive relationships lie in ourselves, not in the environment. We assume incorrectly that the people around us will not like us, do not have the time, aren't interested in what we are doing or don't want to be helpful. Because of these assumptions, we don't ask other people things or initiate contact with them. We create a self-fulfilling prophecy. We never find out that our assumptions about other people aren't true, because we never check them out.

The best rule for extending support networks is to seek out other people. Sometimes they won't want to help or do things, but that is not the only response we will receive. Sometimes other people seem to enjoy contact and exchange with you, and even enjoy taking the time to help you. Also, they will then begin to seek your help, which will balance out the relationship. When people begin to reach out to others, almost invariably they find that people are friendly, easy to approach and helpful.

Another way to extend support is to extend the amount and degree of your social contacts. If you are in the habit of eating lunch or dinner alone, begin to invite others to join you. Studies of successful workers, and workers who cope well with stress, show that they usually cultivate a large number of other people in the workplace. Then, when a position becomes open, or information about a delicate subject is needed, that person can tap into his or her social network.

It's not what you know but who you know. You can start by knowing other people in your field, utilizing professional organizations and meetings for professional networking.

- Ask people where they work and what they do.
- Strike up conversations with co-workers about their civic or social interests.
- Imagine yourself as a host to the world instead of a guest. Introduce people to each other.
- Make connections anywhere; talk to people in the line at the supermarket or on the bus.

Actively approaching others will set you in the direction of achieving your goals.

Support and Exchange

Social support is not static or fixed. It grows and can be strained or strengthened according to the care that you give your networks. When you do not receive the support you need, there can be many reasons. It is possible that you have a lot of support available to you, but you are not willing to receive it. Or, you may not have much support in your ongoing relationships, but know where to reach out for it. Look at social support as an exchange of energy from one person to another.

People do not exist independently of one another; they participate in many varieties of relationships. Difficulties occur in the area of social support when an imbalance in this energy exchange occurs. Since most people do not keep elaborate track of each exchange of support, it is possible to get out of balance when you have given too much and not taken back enough support to keep going. Even cars have to stop for tune-ups.

Two other areas of exchange help to rebalance your life: self-support—things you do for yourself—and receiving care from others. People often feel more comfortable with one method of exchange and concentrate their activities in that direction.

Research and common sense suggest that we manage stress best when we participate actively in all three types of exchange. The two other areas of exchange are discussed in greater depth in Chapter 4. They are mentioned here as reminders that social support is one part of a complex of exchange and renewal mechanisms.

BUILDING SUPPORT THROUGH PERSONAL NETWORKING

In times of transition, crisis or extreme pressure, the best coping strategy is often mobilizing a personal network.

For example, imagine you are job hunting. One way to do it is to call the network of people you know who are in your field or who might know people in your area, who in turn might be aware of a job. A few phone calls mobilize your network by making people aware that you have a need. You will also gather useful information and a further set of contacts. Thus, a friend might tell you that she has an ex-roommate who works at a certain company that she heard was looking for a marketing person. Career development consultants say that for each person, the right job lies about three links along this chain.

Networks and chains of connections are the primary way that things get done in society. This is also the way that information is transferred. Unlike formal organizational structures, networks are formless, extensive, amorphous and infinitely flexible.

Think about your own organization. You will probably notice that the people who are most effective at their work are often those with large informal networks within the organization. They know how to get things done and find things out. They have friends in every division and they do favors for others. In turn they can count on others for help.

Networks thrive on balance. The degree to which others see you as helpful, as a good resource and as supportive determines how they will respond to your needs. Generally, the most effective networks are those which flow in both directions.

Let us say that you have a problem, which is a source of pressure or stress in your life. Personal networking is a helpful way to move toward solution.

EXERCISE 17

- Write down a pressing problem on a piece of paper. List all the people who you know, even slightly, who might be a resource for this problem. This includes people who might have relevant information, people who have been through similar situations or people who might relate to or have something to do with your problem. Think about how each of them might be helpful.

_____

_____

_____

_____

_____

_____

_____

_____

- Begin to contact each of them, discuss your difficulty or need and ask for help. Be sure to let them know what you need, or what sort of help they might be able to offer. Few people are willing to enter into vague or open-ended commitments.

Differences Between Men and Women

Just as each individual's support network is composed of different people in the various groupings, there are also differences in the way men and women compose their networks. On the whole it seems that women know more about developing their support networks and making use of them.

In *Intimate Strangers,* Lillian Rubin provides numerous examples of this pattern. Rubin found that women share their deepest secrets, while men rarely confide in each other. Men list fewer relationships than women, and their friendships have a different content and quality than those described by women. Women talk more about feelings and personal experience, while men give more information and share opinions more than women. Male relationships are based more on a shared activity, like a sport or job, whereas women's relationships tend to focus on more sensitive life events.

Two-thirds of the single men Rubin interviewed were unable to name a best friend, and when they did have a friend it was likely to be a woman. There are some differences with married couples. Married women tend to resume their intimate friendships with women after marriage, while men tend to develop an intimate relationship with their spouse. This may explain some of the research findings that report the benefits of being married for men—they are able to create more intimate relationships within the framework of marriage.

Men benefit from a different sort of network. From their school days in team sports through various clubs, organizations and fraternities, men form fraternal and friendship groups. These groups perform many functions, in addition to socializing and blowing off steam. The *old boy network* forms a resource pool of potential recruits for jobs, information, services and other activities. This is useful and helpful for those who are "in," but penalizes those who are not part of these informal, often long-standing, networks.

As they enter the executive market, women have begun to form their own *old girl networks* to offer themselves these same advantages. The extent of these networks is critial to many personal needs. For example, if one needs a lawyer or contractor, or wants to know something about government regulations or is looking for a new job, this kind of network is the first one that is consulted. Many jobs, bits of information and opportunities travel almost exclusively along such networks. Not being connected to some of them is a handicap, and can make coping with any pressure or difficulty harder.

Ideas for Generating Support

This chapter has explored ways to mobilize and expand the effectiveness of your personal support networks. Following are general guidelines to increase the effectiveness of your personal support networks:

- Ask for direct help and be receptive when it is offered.
- List six people with whom you would like to improve your relationship and one action step you will be willing to take toward this improvement.
- Rid yourself of relationships that are not supportive or are damaging to you.
- Maintain high-quality relationships on and off the job by telling them how much you value their support.
- Review your present network, make an honest assessment of how well it is working for you and identify areas where you could use some changes.
- Keep your energy exchange balanced; return favors and thoughtfulness.

RENEWING YOURSELF

Chapter Four

SELF-RENEWAL: RECONNECTING WITH YOURSELF

Stress often stems from a lack of awareness, consideration and respect for our feelings, needs, values and life goals. This chapter initiates a process of self-reflection, introducing exercises for learning about dimensions of ourselves that we neglect, or that are simply out of our everyday awareness. Whether or not we pay attention to these, they affect our lives. But when stress lies outside of our awareness and consideration, we feel helpless and controlled by what we do and experience, and we miss opportunities to bring our lives into harmony with our internal needs, goals and values.

People are not machines that can be pushed to high performance. When we push ourselves to accomplish something, and we experience resistance, we need to ask ourselves why we are doing this, why it is important to us. Burnout and distress are sometimes a message from our bodies that we need to explore these basic questions. The symptoms signal not an inability to manage the outside world, but a disconnection within ourselves. So the processes of preventing and overcoming burnout and performing up to our capacities involve external management of difficult situations and working together with others, as well as inner reflection on such questions as who we are, what we need and what we want from our lives. We also need to take proper care of ourselves—physically, emotionally and spiritually—and replenish the energy we expend each day. These processes of going within and regenerating ourselves make up the activities that we call "self-renewal."

When we notice signs of burnout, or when we reach a point of transition through a job loss or other life change, it is a good time for a reassessment of where we are, where we have come from and where we are going. In the early 1960s, management consultants like Herb Shepard began to offer executive seminars in "Life Planning." In these retreats, participants explored where they were in their lives. After reassessment, they planned and executed changes.

After these workshops, executives reported positive changes in their personal lives and in their feelings about themselves, and in their performance at work. Through knowing where they were in life and where they might be going, they could reconnect in a more positive and creative way to their work. As a result of the workshop, others make important life changes—changing jobs, taking up new hobbies and activities, and reorienting their relationships.

Self-exploration and self-understanding are the cornerstones of self-renewal. They are also antidotes for burnout and excessive life stress. Unless we are self-aware, we are out of touch with important guidance concerning correct decisions, and we lack a sense of purpose and direction. In such a state, even ordinary pressures and demands can confuse and immobilize us.

When we are feeling pressured or dissatisfied, it is a natural reflex to look around to try to discover the source of the stress. We look in the environment or in the people around us. There is an illusory sense of relief when we can blame our condition on something, even if the act of blaming leads us nowhere. Usually the reason that blaming leads us nowhere is that by looking outside ourselves we neglect the one constant in every situation—ourselves.

The human being is composed of a vast inner conscious and unconscious world of often competing desires, feelings, thoughts, skills, goals and expectations. Our rich capacity for self-awareness and our capacity to plan and act on our images and creative aspirations lead to the richness of human life and also to its pain and difficulty. Often the burnout we feel in a job is not due to the work situation itself, but to our idealistic expectations or our personal needs. Self-management begins not with control over the external world, but with an expansion of our awareness of our inner worlds.

WHO AM I: EXPLORING THE PERSON WITHIN

Stress, distress and burnout are all signs of conflict. Conflict can exist on many levels—between personal needs and the demands of the employer, between people, between groups of people and between different factions within the self.

One of the major sources of personal stress is the way the organization treats individuals. Some organizations assume that people are interchangeable, that they need to be tightly controlled to perform and that their feelings are irrelevant. These assumptions conflict with the way most of us experience ourselves. Stress and later burnout come about from trying to fit into the straitjacket of the organization's inadequate model of human nature.

Often, burnout and distress have to do with difficulties in our understanding and respect for our inner selves and potentialities. These assumptions are:

Each person contains a vast inner world of thoughts, feelings, values, aspirations, potentials and needs that he or she is capable of knowing and exploring. Distress, ill health and burnout can result from neglecting this inner world. We need to explore and connect to ourselves on this complex level and to take this world into account in all of our actions. We need to act in reflection of these inner values, needs and messages.

Each person has a vast potential, which he or she rarely lives up to, and a complex multifaceted nature. Full and healthy living must respect our many facets and reflect and express as many of our potentials as possible.

People live in a world with others, and they need to feel connected, validated, helped, involved and trusting in their relationships. To get what we want and become who we want to be, we need to become deeply involved with others. People are communal; solitary people seem to have difficulty with their health and well-being. Other people let us know of our value, and confirm and validate our sense of worth and identity. To feel safe in the world, we need to trust others.

The person is continually changing, evolving, growing and becoming. Each of us is molded by past experience and habits, but we are ever changing. Much of our change is self-generated and self-created in the direction of our goals. We make choices every moment to act or not act, and we need to take responsibility for the directions we choose. People are not entirely molded by their environments or constraints, but always have the possibility of creative and novel choices and solutions to difficulties.

PERSONAL NEEDS

There are many things a human being needs to remain alive. This includes air, food and shelter. In addition, people need the following to grow and thrive. They need:

- Other people for companionship, love and personal support
- To establish and maintain a healthy self-esteem
- To be competent
- To be challenged
- To achieve
- To have transcendent and spiritual connections
- To find meaning and purpose in living

When you complete Exercise 18, Needs Assessment, you will have created a diagram of your needs and priorities. If you are not feeling satisfied in some of the areas listed, you may discover that you are experiencing stress.

EXERCISE 18 — NEEDS ASSESSMENT

Listed below are some of the important personal needs. For each type of need indicate how important or pressing it is for you, and how satisfied you are in that area in your current life.

Type of Need	Importance			Satisfaction		
	Lo	Med	Hi	Lo	Med	Hi
Sexuality						
Friendship						
Being Loved						
Loving Others						
Self-Esteem						
Creative Achievement						
Religious Experience, Spirituality						
Respect of Peers						
Excitement, Challenge						
Quiet, Peacefulness						

Psychologist Abraham Maslow suggested that not all people feel all needs with the same urgency at the same time. Maslow proposed that at certain times in one's life certain needs are the paramount. A young person might be most concerned about a lack of a deep intimate relationship and less focused on other needs.

Maslow also observed that many basic needs seemed to be met for most people, and that as these needs were met, other types of needs—for such things as personal growth and creative self-expression—became important. For example, since most of us have enough to eat, food is rarely a concern for us. In a poor country, concern about physcial survival is paramount.

The needs for other people, for achievement and for a meaningful life seem to be most important for people today. These are the needs that are unmet, or inadequately met, for many people. When some basic needs are frustrated, the body usually responds with the psychophysiological stress response. Over time, with continual frustration, stress builds up and various physical and emotional difficulties arise.

Because frustration of basic needs is one of the messages of burnout and stress, we begin our internal self-exploration with an inquiry into your experience of what needs are most central to you right now, and how well they are satisfied.

SELF-ESTEEM

One central human need is for self-esteem—to experience ourselves positively, to feel competent and effective at what we do, to feel cared for and valued, and to feel good about who we are. When we feel good about ourselves, we act differently than we do when we feel threatened, disliked and not valued. When we have high self-esteem, we feel good, confident and creative. Cultivation and enhancement of self-esteem are, therefore, necessary for our well-being.

Self-esteem is not something we have or don't have. It *is* something that can be developed; we can create situations and act in such a way that it grows and flourishes. There are several sources of self-esteem: achievements, power and influence over events and people, feeling accepted, valued and cared for by people we value; and acting consistently with personal values.

The reverse is also true. Self-esteem declines when we abdicate our personal power, when we do not connect to the people around us, and when we do not articulate and act on our core values and beliefs. Sources of self-esteem are almost identical to the activities that help people manage their lives, overcome stress and burnout and achieve personal effectiveness.

Consider to what degree each of the potential sources of self-esteem are operative in your life now.

- For each source, ask yourself if you enhance your self-esteem in that way. Your sense of self-esteem will probably derive more from one or two of the areas.

- Think about the different spheres of your life—work, family, friends and you alone. Which sources of self-esteem are experienced in each one? For example, do you derive your sense of acceptance more from your family and experience power and achievement in your work?

Open and Defensive Behavior

It is interesting to think about our encounters with other people in terms of self-esteem. Every interaction has some effect on the self-esteem of the people involved. Many of our interactions are even intended to support our self-esteem. For example, we like to be seen positively, so we avoid offending other people and sometimes even avoid telling them bad news or being honest about mistakes we have made. Most people tend to blame circumstances or other people for mistakes; this is partly an attempt to salvage self-esteem.

When we look at interaction in terms of self-esteem, we can see two intentions that lie behind our behavior. We can relate defensively—acting primarily to protect our feelings of self-worth from real or imagined harm—or openly—sharing our true feelings and being open to those of the other person. In every interaction, we can sense to what degree we are open or defensive. When we see ourselves acting defensively, we need to look at what we are trying to protect ourselves from. Many times, we are defending ourselves from a threat that is more imagined than real.

People work best when the people around them validate their value and worth. When people around us support our self-esteem, we feel more trust and become more open and effective. Much of the stress and burnout that occur in work settings (and in families) stem from interactions that do not validate self-esteem.

Defensive settings are ineffective, both at getting work done and in supporting personal well-being. Here is what happens. People do not support each other's positive worth. They criticize, backbite and withhold compliments. Each person feels bad and becomes more defensive—withholding important information, covering up problems and mistakes, and avoiding responsibility. Over time, people begin to feel more powerless, unsupported, lonely and frustrated. Things get worse and worse.

Another outcome results when one key person in a work group begins to set up interactions that validate and support people's self-esteem. The person who supports others receives better responses from the people nearby, who in turn feel better and do better work. Trust builds and people begin to be more supportive and validating of each other.

EXERCISE 19

In this exercise you will explore your personal sense of identity. Take some time to answer the question "Who am I?"

- Write at least twenty, wide-ranging answers—list roles, feelings, things you like to do, qualities that reflect essential aspects of yourself.

1. _____
2. _____
3. _____
4. _____
5. _____
6. _____
7. _____
8. _____
9. _____
10. _____

11. _____
12. _____
13. _____
14. _____
15. _____
16. _____
17. _____
18. _____
19. _____
20. _____

- Look over your list. Notice that no single definition or answer encompasses the whole of you. You are much more than even all of the answers.

- Go over your list once more. Renumber the answers in terms of those most important to you.

- Which answers touch closest to the core of who you are?

_____

_____

_____

- Which answers are less important?

_____

_____

_____

- Look at each answer again, beginning with the most important. Where, how and when do you express these qualities or aspects of yourself? Think of some other ways that you can express each of these qualities. Write these down.

_____

_____

_____

The degree to which a setting supports the self-esteem of the people in it is critical to personal self-worth and also to its effectiveness. Things that support people's sense of worth and psychological well-being also encourage health and optimal performance.

EXPLORING OURSELVES

You can think of each aspect of yourself and your personality as a different self. That is, you can take a quality or facet and explore it as if it is a being that lives within you. Instead of seeing yourself as a single, unified whole, it is more realistic to think of yourself as a kind of loose confederation of different selves, each with its own place and purpose.

Philosopher James Ogilvy and psychiatrist Robert Jay Lifton both point out that instead of looking for a single core identity, people today need to see themselves as what Lifton calls "protean"—many-faceted, many-identified people who are in flux and developing in new ways. We can expect to change jobs several times in our lives, and even to be in different intimate relationships, live in different places and have a variety of involvements and interests.

One way to divide up our different identities is through different aspects of conscious experience. We have several modes for experiencing ourselves and the world. These modes include body sensing, thinking, feeling and action.

EXERCISE 20

Take a moment now to turn your attention inward and see that you have direct sensation from your body, that you are also having thoughts and feelings, and that you can act and experience your behavior and its consequences.

- Think about how and where you experience each of the selves that lie within you. Which of them are more familiar to you?

_____

_____

_____

- Which are less often used?

  _____

  _____

  _____

- How can you explore your body self, your thinking self, your feeling self and your action self?

  _____

  _____

  _____

- Think of different aspects of your daily life. When does each of these selves come into play?

  _____

  _____

  _____

- Which ones might you consult more frequently, or look at more?

  _____

  _____

  _____

For many of us, especially those who face stress-related problems, difficulties stem from neglect of our body self or our feeling self. Think of ways to pay more attention to the facets of yourself you are neglecting.

Pressure, distress, dissatisfaction and burnout can result from a life that reflects only a narrow slice of who you are. For example, a person who has a routine job and a rich family life, or is involved in a variety of community activities or has a complex and demanding hobby, will probably experience less burnout and dissatisfaction on that job than a person who has very little to look forward to when he or she leaves work. The more of ourself that we express and the more that we express our many qualities and potentials, the less frustrated and burned out we will be.

Think back over your life and remember things that you have done, things that you sometime thought you'd like to do, things that you have stopped doing, things you have never done. Remember how you felt doing those things or how much you wanted to do them.

- Ask yourself why you didn't do them, or stopped doing them. You may think, "I don't have time for them" or "I don't know anybody to do them with" or some similar excuse.

- Now, imagine how your life would be enriched and broadened by including some of these activities.

- List several activities that you might begin doing.

_____

_____

_____

_____

_____

_____

_____

There are difficulties involved in actualizing our multifaceted nature. Life does not become richer just because we do more things. We need to find balance and make choices about what to express and act on. Time and life are finite, and our interests and possibilities are infinite. We need to make choices and set limits.

Some of the conflict in our lives is caused by differences between the actual and the possible, between the way we appear and the way we are. When these differences are too great, the gaps can be a source of distress.

Below is a list of some of the types of differences that lead to conflict.

- On each side of the page, list a few phrases that describe yourself along that dimension:

DESCRIBE YOURSELF

Me at Work _____

_____

_____

_____

Me at Home _____

_____

_____

_____

The Roles I Play _____

_____

_____

_____

The Person I Really Am _____

_____

_____

_____

How Others See Me _____

_____

_____

_____

How I See Myself _____

_____

_____

_____

How I Am _____

_____

_____

_____

How I'd Like to Be _____

_____

_____

_____

- As you look at the differences along these dimensions, imagine what it would feel like if each of these areas were more congruent.

- What steps could you take to make yourself more integrated?

_____

_____

_____

- Are these changes worth it to you?

_____

MYTHS AND ROLES

Many people create stress by maintaining unrealistic expectations of themselves. They expect themselves to accomplish the impossible. A person may be evaluating his or her behavior in terms of "shoulds." For example, he may say that a good employee should always finish all the work he is assigned, or a good husband should always be ready to help out around the house or a friend should always be available to help a person who is upset. The myth of what an employee, boss, parent, spouse or friend *should be* leads us to expect more than we have to offer, or leads us to criticize our efforts as inadequate.

EXERCISE 23

- Write down your major roles or identities—at work, in your family or in the community.

_____

_____

_____

- For each role, write down some of the things that you expect yourself to do in that position.

_____

_____

_____

_____

_____

- Ask yourself if these are what you expect of yourself in these roles. And, if you fall short, what do you say or do to yourself?

_____

_____

_____

_____

Much of our daily stress comes from not living up to our expectations. Usually we expect much more from ourselves than the people in our work site or family expect of us.

MOVING THROUGH LIFE

THE PERSON IN PROCESS

We live in the present. Yet, at this moment we are the total of all the events and experiences of our past, and are also determined by our vision of our future and our hopes and goals. The first lesson in self-exploration and life planning requires stepping back from the present and looking at your life as an evolving whole.

EXERCISE 24

This graphic represents your life line. All life lines are different—they're shaped by different events, actions or decisions. The left edge of the graphic represents your birth, and the right edge your death. In between is the "now" line.

Your Life Line

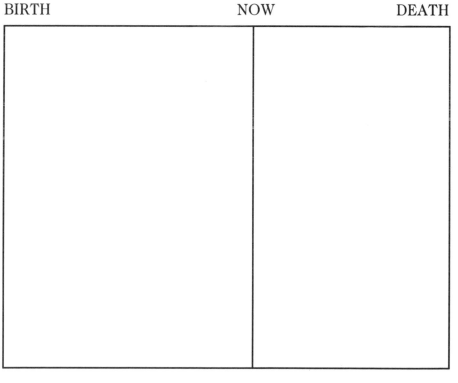

BIRTH   NOW   DEATH

- Draw your life line as follows, in pencil (so you can make changes): write the significant events in your life—important changes, transitions, crises, moves, illnesses—in the interval between your birth and today.

Write the positive or exciting events toward the top of the chart and the stressful or negative events toward the bottom edge. You are entering the highs, lows and changes in your life so far. Include events happening to you, as well as significant events in your family and, if you wish, significant social/political events.

Draw a line that connects the events, moving up and down, to represent the emotional climate and progression of your life.

Divide your life into a series of phases or periods that make sense to you. For example, your college education, your first marriage, job, or time living in one place.

Now envision possible futures. Fill in the one you would like to see between the "now" line and your death, with hypothetical significant events.

Continue your life line, projecting yourself into the future.

How many of the actions that shaped your life line resulted from choices you made, and how many from choices others made for you?

_____

_____

_____

Is there evidence of action you've taken without really making a decision—that is, something you did simply because it was expected of you?

_____

_____

_____

Put the following symbols along your life line. Put ! where you took the greatest risk. Place *X* where you encountered an obstacle preventing you from getting or doing what you wanted. Use *O* to locate a critical decision that was made for you by someone else. Put + at the point of the best decision you ever made and — at the worst decision you made. Finally, put ? where you see a critical or important decision coming up in the future.

Consider your life line carefully now, complete with symbols:

Have you learned anything that surprises you? _____

_____

How have decisions affected the shape of your life line?

_____

_____

Did you actually make the decisions that affected your life?

_____

_____

LIFE GOALS

Imagine facing a difficult and stressful situation in a job or family that is important and meaningful to you. Whatever the situation, you will probably find the energy to face the problem and do your best to resolve it. Now imagine you have a job or live with people whose general welfare or goals do not coincide with yours. The struggle with the stressful situation will be that much greater.

The phenomenon of burnout has several roots. One is the extent to which the place you work, or the people you live with, share your goals. Second, there is the degree to which you feel that you can actively pursue those goals. Do you feel a sense of power?

One of the primary causes of burnout and inability to manage stress is working or living in a setting without clear goals or feeling able to meet your goals. A situation is supportive when all the people working or living there have a large area of shared commitments and goals, and when all the people are involved in them. When individual goals are far away from the group goals (for example, people are working only for their salaries, not caring about what the organization produces), burnout and added stress result, and it is harder to marshal the energy to overcome difficulties.

Some people have life goals yet do not feel they have the power to achieve them. Or, they feel blocked by their environment. Sometimes if we cannot achieve our goals in one setting, we must make the decision to leave and try another place. Other times we must take risks to make changes. Some risks succeed, some fail. However, when we feel helpless and do not make changes to achieve our goals, the resulting stagnation produces great stress and burnout.

Now complete Exercise 25, your Personal Inventory.

EXERCISE 25 — PERSONAL GOAL INVENTORY

In each area of your life, what are your major, specific goals? Try to be concrete. Don't think about how you want to feel (e.g., happy, challenged), but what you want to happen in the next few years and how it could come about. Relax and imagine a future in which, over the next few years, you are working toward your goals. The more details you can imagine in your future, the more likely you are to discover ways to bring it about. Write these in the Specific Goals column below.

Think of the major obstacles to realizing your goals. Often they lie within the setting, or you experience resistance from people around you. Think clearly about the specific obstacles to realizing what you want. Write these in the Obstacles to Achieving Them column.

Imagine several immediate, active steps you can take to empower yourself and to begin working to overcome the obstacles. Be concrete and specific. Write these in the Steps to Be Taken to Achieve column.

Area of Life	Specific Goals	Obstacles to Achieving Them	Steps to Be Taken to Achieve
Current Job			
Career			
Family			

Area of Life	Specific Goals	Obstacles to Achieving Them	Steps to Be Taken to Achieve
Friendships			
Spiritual/Religious			
Play			
Personal Growth			
Community/Political			
Other Areas			

What fears do you have about taking the risks necessary to reach your goals? Inability to formulate and work toward personal goals creates stress because it robs a person of a reason to overcome challenges and deal with frustration. The more meaningful the goal, the more life energy and support a person can muster to overcome difficulty.

BALANCING ENERGY AND CONFLICT

Work and Family

The greatest and most difficult conflicts many of us will ever experience are those between work and family. These take two forms: first we have to divide our priorities, commitments, time and energy between work and family/personal involvements; second, there are conflicts between members of a household, especially concerning a couple's differing levels of commitment to work or family.

Any conflict causes pressure and distress. Often, we can't find a way to make ourselves fully satisfied, or to satisfy ourselves and our spouse. Added to this, recent changes in sex roles, such as the restructuring of household expectations, parental responsibilities and women entering previously male-dominated work settings, have required even old agreements and solutions to be renegotiated.

Tragically, working people often make their family and personal relationships their lowest priority. Yet people who are successful at managing stress and remaining healthy are often those who make their personal and family lives a priority and are able to say "no" to outside demands.

EXERCISE 26 — EXPLORING YOUR ENERGY COMMITMENTS

In the graph below, indicate the amount of energy and time you give to work, play, relating to friends and family, and to yourself.

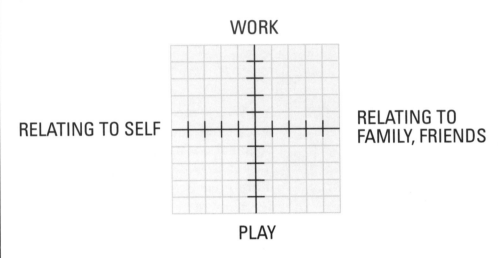

Now, indicate how much energy you would like to devote to each of these areas.

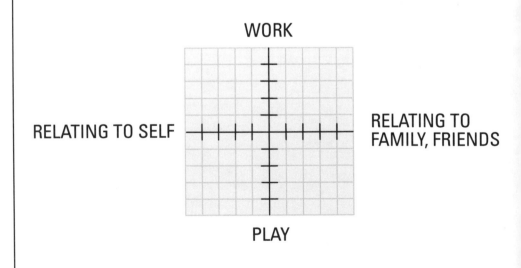

Write down some of the activities you do in each domain of your life. Then, add some of the ones you would like to do or think you might want to do.

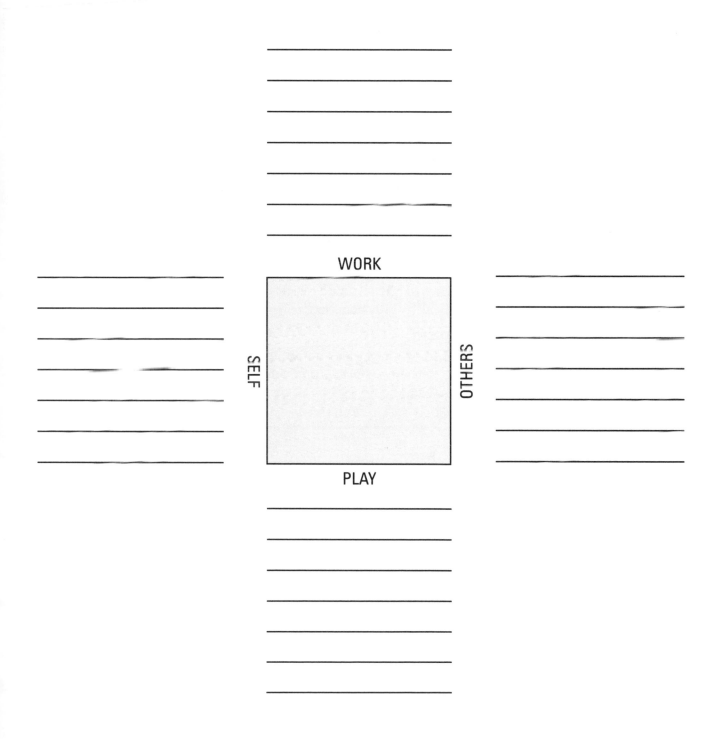

EXERCISE 27 — ENERGY BALANCE

The essential concept of self-care is balance. Our various needs must be balanced, and our own needs must balance with those of others.

Like any organism, the human being is a system that exchanges energy with its environment. We take in various forms of energy—air, food, experience, and contact with others—and we also give energy out—exhalation, excretion, communication, action and personal support.

In looking at our energy balance, we need to explore the various modes of action we engage in. Activity differs in terms of the source of motivation and also the direction it takes. The source can be *intrinsic*—doing things because we want to—or *extrinsic*—doing things because we feel we should, or ought to, or have to do them. The direction of activity can be *giving*—doing things for others—or *receiving*—allowing others to do things for and to us.

None of these modes is in itself right or wrong, or healthy or unhealthy. Rather, people who feel good about themselves and manage stress well have a balance of energy in each area.

Fill in your regular activities in the appropriate quadrant below. See which areas predominate in your life, and which are less usual.

Receiving	Intrinsic
Things done to and for you by others _____ _____ _____ _____	Things you do because you want to _____ _____ _____ _____
Extrinsic	**Giving**
Things you do because you "should," "have to" or "ought to" _____ _____ _____ _____	Things you do to and for others _____ _____ _____ _____

The other area of conflict, often more severe, is between the two people in a couple. Each has a different interpretation or need for time together, and each has different priorities. Balancing two careers, or finding time to be together when one is on the *fast track* at work, is difficult. Couples that solve these dilemmas are clear and open about each other's needs and commitments, share information and feelings, and are flexible in compromising or looking for something other than win/lose solutions.

CURRENT LIFE EXPLORATION

As part of your life planning and self-renewal process, explore where you are right now, and look ahead at some choices and changes that you might want to make. Exercises 25, 26 and 27 served as guides for your reflections on your current life situation.

The following questions allow you to jot down some of your thoughts on each theme—you don't need to have a complete answer; life is continually changing. The purpose is to make your feelings about your life more explicit, and to define some areas and dimensions of your life that need renewed energy or redefined commitment.

- What are my current concerns and worries?
- What are the greatest pressures on me right now? When do I feel it? What must I do about it?
- What is changing in my life?
- What are the major values or goals that I would like to achieve in my life?
- What are the most important payoffs or rewards that I am looking for in my life?
- What intense, gratifying and deeply meaningful experiences have I had in my life? What sorts of peak experiences would I like to have in the future?
- What are the major constraints or limits that I experience in my life right now, that make it difficult to achieve the rewards, goals and experiences I seek?

- What are the major obstacles to getting what I want out of life? (Divide them into obstacles that lie inside you and those are external. Think of some of the ways you can change or diminish the force of these obstacles.)

- What are the things I do well? List them.

- What are the things that I do poorly? Would I like to improve my ability in these areas or stop doing these things?

- What would I like to stop doing?

- What would I like to start doing or learn to do?

- What are the central goals in my life right now? What were my goals five years ago? What do I project will be my goals five years from now?

- Which of the things that I do regularly do I expect to do less often in the following years? What new things do I expect to have to do, or want to do?

- What is the most important change or crisis that I expect to face in the next decade?

- What is the most important choice I will have to make in the next few years?

- Which domain of my life (work, family, friends, self) is the central one right now? In the next five years, which domains do I expect to become more and less important in my life?

- What ideal futures can I anticipate? (Imagine what you would like to experience, what you would like to be doing, and who or what kind of people you would like to be doing things with.)

- Imagine it is some time in the future and you have just died. Write your obituary as the person in your life who is closest to you might write it. What do you expect you will be remembered for? What sort of achievements do you expect to have?

CAREER EXPLORATION

Now take a moment to focus on the role your career plays in your life.

- What facets of my career do I enjoy most or find most meaningful?
- What facets of my career do I like least?
- Where in my work do I find the greatest challenge?
- What skills, talents and abilities do I bring to my job?
- What skills, talents and abilities could my work potentially allow me to develop?
- What do I want out of my work, what benefits and rewards?
- What led me to choose the type of work I do? What values and personal feelings led me to this type of work?
- How has my work been unsatisfying, or how has my satisfaction with my work diminished?
- What new areas, skills and types of work would I like to pursue? What prevents me from going in one of these directions?
- What is the greatest frustation and difficulty in my work? What would I most like to change about my work?

CREATING CHANGE IN YOUR LIFE

There is no simple set of instructions for proceeding with a personal change process. Some people can reflect and then begin to plan and implement changes. Others work with the people closest to them—family and friends—to create changes. Still others vacillate back and forth, either because they are not clear what to change or because they cannot find the energy to motivate them to begin.

Change represents a very deep commitment and consequential decision. It should not be done impulsively or initiated too quickly. First, select an area of your life in which you would like to see change. Then, spend time, as you have done in several other areas already, imagining concretely and specifically alternative possibilities. When you envision concretely, you begin to see consequences and have the opportunity to experience what the projected change would be like in your life. Many times, the envisioning process helps you see unintended consequences, or lack of clarity in your decisions or plans.

The generation of alternate possibilities and directions, a sort of list of possible pathways, is critical to change. Often, merely setting ourselves free from the way things are now and envisioning or thinking about how things can be different, is a highly creative act. We see things that we never looked at before. As you generate alternatives, let them come up without criticism. When you have a large list of possibilities, try to explore their possible consequences and results. Very often, this portion of planning and changing can be done best with the people closest to you.

The methods of change are up to you. Many people use personal counseling or psychotherapy. Many of the exercises and techniques in this book are derived from therapeutic processes. The newer styles of psychotherapy espouse the growth model of human potential outlined at the start of this chapter, which sees counseling as personal guidance to help people reach their unique potential and creativity.

Change does not require counseling or therapy. It requires a clear decision and a personal will to take risks and attempt new behavior. It often involves practicing new skills and learning new methods of response, as you have done in this book. Given the range of possibilities and the shifting demands of our lives, a person who does not welcome change and learn new things will be seriously handicapped.

Chapter Five

ATTUNEMENT: SKILLS FOR ATTAINING RELAXATION AND PHYSICAL WELLNESS

The body, like any organization, is a self-regulating system. Both physical and organizational systems have boundaries with the outside world, and have internal processes that manage the flow of materials, resources, services and information. Both systems develop, growing more complex over time, and are continually threatened by change. Either a person or an organization can act self-destructively, causing damage by ineffective action, and perhaps die. Both types of systems need to grow and develop while at the same time maintaining and renewing themselves.

The key to self-renewing, whether within an organization or within a person, lies in the level of awareness of threats, and the strategies for dealing with them. Organisms must be vigilant and take care of themselves. Physiologically this means taking care of all physical systems, replenishing them with rest and reenergizing them, exchanging energy and resources with others, and becoming aware of difficulty early enough to exercise corrective reaction. While many people know how to do these things organizationally—using strategic planning, market research and quality control to remain aware—they do not exercise the same care and awareness when it comes to their bodies.

If we are not aware of small fluctuations in a system, they grow. Consider, for example, the buildup of muscle tension when under stress. Muscles become chronically tense over a day, and we become less and less sensitive to this tension. We go home and move something that would ordinarily be manageable, and we accidentally strain our back. Was the strain caused by moving the table, or by lack of awareness and lack of corrective response to release the growing tension?

We need to heed the messages of our body to maintain health and use our natural physiological resources to resist stress, overcome burnout and prevent illness. As a result, stress and burnout are largely preventable.

The first line of defense against the physical symptoms caused by stress is effective regular care of the body. The body must be kept flexible, rested, responsive, energized, aware of itself and prepared to meet demands. This means getting enough sleep, eating well, exercising and releasing the tension that builds up each day through relaxation techniques.

WELLNESS, ILLNESS AND TENSION

A healthy, vital, creative and fulfilling life is within our grasp. How do we remain healthy? The first thought many people have is medical insurance. If you become ill, you want to be certain that the most modern, up-to-date medical expertise and technology is available. And you want to be sure that saving your life will not ruin your prosperity and your family's economic future.

As we reflect further on our health, we see that being healthy is much more than simply the absence of illness. Health involves a feeling of vitality, of energy, of ability to do what we want to do, of involvement in meaningful activity. In short, *health* involves the entire quality of our lives.

The question facing each of us is how much is our health within our control. Is health, prosperity or wisdom a matter of chance or the result of factors beyond our control? No. Your health is up to you.

THE SEARCH FOR WELLNESS

While it may be true that our body is to some extent a battleground for opposing forces, more often that not we weaken ourselves by undermining our ability to resist disease, and by carelessly ignoring the dangers that face us.

Most disease is preventable and most life stress is manageable. The pain, heart disease, ulcers and even cancer that ruin our lives, threaten our livelihoods and eventually kill us are often unnecessary. While we may still die of a heart attack or cancer, evidence is growing that we can postpone that death or bring it upon ourselves much earlier than nature may have intended. To some extent, health or illness is a choice that each person makes.

EXERCISE 28 — ASSESSING YOUR OWN WELLNESS

How would you rate your overall level of wellness, your state of vitality, health and well-being? Now complete Exercise 28. When you have done so, you will have created a picture of your wellness—now and in the controllable future.

LOW   HIGH
POOR   1   2   3   4   5   6   7   EXCELLENT

Reflect on the things in your life that prevent you from being as well as you would like—the obstacles to optimal health. List at least five of them, beginning with those that most inhibit your health.

1. _____

_____

2. _____

_____

3. _____

_____

4. _____

_____

5. _____

_____

Look over your list and think about the degree to which these obstacles to greater health and well-being are within your control. That is, are there things that you could do to prevent them from doing damage, or to eliminate them from your life? Circle the items on your list that you feel could be changed or overcome.

SYMPTOMS OF STRESS

It is easy to know when we are under too much stress. Minor symptoms like headaches, insomnia, bowel difficulties or muscle tension are signals that pressures have built up to dangerously high levels. Sometimes such symptoms are a response to unusual demands and crises that are soon over— a deadline, an examination, a new job, a family conflict. However, many people experience so much daily tension that the common stress symptoms become a way of life. They are plagued by physical symptoms or emotional distress on a regular basis—perhaps every day. If these symptoms are not taken care of, more serious illness will develop as the body gradually wears down under the pressure.

Assessment 10 lists common physical and emotional symptoms that are due partially to ineffective coping with stress. Think back over the past month. How frequently have you experienced each symptom? If you find that you have a number of symptoms as frequently as every week, you need to do something about them. Of course, if is important to note that while these symptoms are commonly associated with excessive stress, the presence of a symptom can also indicate some specific illness that may have relatively little to do with your life stress. If you have a chronic physical or emotional symptom, have it checked by a doctor.

Having stress-related symptoms is a message from your body that you are not managing the pressure and demands of your life well enough. The symptoms are the end point of a long chain of events that have to do with the demands made upon you, your thoughts and feelings about them, and the way you respond to them.

Your Relationship to Your Body

When we allow stress to build up, we demonstrate that we are out of touch with our bodies. Pain can be thought of as the body shouting for attention because we didn't pay attention to previous gentle signals of pressure or fatigue. Pain is the insistence that we pay attention to our own needs.

Now take some time to complete the following two exercises. They will help you establish your relationship to your body.

- How do you feel about your body?
- Do you like it, dislike it or not think about it very much?
- How much attention and care do you give your body?
- Is your body a friend or an enemy, a source of pleasure or a source of pain and discomfort?
- Explore your answers to these questions.

Broadly, we can describe sets of negative/unhealthy and positive/healthy attitudes toward your body:

Negative: The body is ignored, and its needs or messages are not allowed to enter awareness until serious physical breakdowns or damage have occurred. The body is seen as an enemy, not liked and not expected to be helpful or come through in a crisis. The body gets sick for no apparent reason.

EXERCISE 29

- Write down some of your negative feelings and attitudes toward your body:

_____

_____

_____

_____

_____

Positive: The body is a friend, whom we know well and can count on for help under reasonable circumstances. If we become ill, we know that we have the resources to become well, and we participate in the healing process. We listen to our bodies, respond to them and respect their needs. The body is a source of pleasure and positive feelings, which are meaningful parts of our lives. We live in our body as much as we do in our mind, and find that our life is a balance of the two influences, a working partnership.

- Write down some of your positive feelings and attitudes toward your body:

_____

_____

_____

_____

_____

_____

Managing stress begins when we make a commitment to develop a positive attitude toward our body. That means using our body to bring us pleasure, and respecting both its wisdom in warning us of difficulty and stress, and its needs. If we pay attention to our bodies, we have gone a long way toward keeping stress from silently slipping into our lives and causing damage. We can spot stress-related difficulty early and reverse it quickly.

WHEN STRESS BUILDS UP

Think back to the last time you had a headache or other painful symptom of stress. Were you aware of tension building up earlier around your scalp and temple?

It is much easier to prevent a headache from occurring in the first place than to get rid of it when it has reached the severe pain level. If we can recognize the early signs, we can take a break—a walk, time out, a short relaxation period—and probably prevent it.

We can learn to listen to our bodies, and when we recognize signs of tension, use that as a signal to do something to bring us back into balance or change our pace. Too often, we react to early signs of stress by telling ourselves that we just have to push harder, as if we are in a race and can beat our headache and finish the job. We think that pushing ourselves makes us more efficient but, in fact, a few short—even three-minute—breaks can give us energy and renewed ability.

Explore what your body is saying to you right now. Check in with your body several times a day. You can become aware of your body's subtle messages—even, one researcher has shown, the firing of one of our billions of nerve cells! Body awareness is a cornerstone of self-care. No physician can always know when something is wrong. Many serious ailments are caught in time or are prevented by people who are sensitive to their bodies.

Ineffective Methods of Managing Tension

At the end of a stressful day we all have ways to relax and unwind. Some of them are healthy and pleasurable—a picnic with the family, a game of tennis or a quiet evening with a person you care for. The day's tension needs to be discharged or else we run the risk of stress-related illnesses developing within our stress-weakened body—chronic headaches, ulcers or high blood pressure, for example. We make ourselves vulnerable to all manner of ailments by not discharging our daily buildup of tension.

Read over the activities listed in Assessment 11. Unfortunately, many of these activities, which we commonly use to unwind, are not helpful. Some, like an occasional beer or aspirin, are probably not too damaging. Others—smoking, for example—do little to overcome daily tension, but quickly become a habit that undermines our health. The key is balance. Any habit that we use to excess can add to our stress and further harm our health.

METHODS OF RELAXATION

We have been exploring ineffective methods of relieving tension. Now, think about the positive things that you do to relax. There is no single effective way to relax. Effective relaxation means that when you are aware of tension building up in your body, you take immediate steps to bring your body back into balance and rest. The tension that builds up may be either physical, mental or a combination of both. There are several types of relaxation activities.

RESTS AND DIVERSIONS

These include taking short naps, reading, seeing movies or spending pleasant time with your family. Rests or diversions are very important; people who do not know how to rest and let their mind leave their work or pressures have no outlet to escape or relieve tension.

Active Physical Exercise

People need exercise, otherwise their muscles, including the critically important heart muscle, deteriorate. Regular exercise increases your body's energy and resiliency, and helps create a feeling of well-being. The exercise you select depends on your personal preference. However, forms of aerobic exercise may be more helpful in exercising the heart, and might be indicated if you have high blood pressure or heart disease.

Now, log your relaxation exercises in Exercise 31.

EXERCISE 31 — ACTIVITIES THAT PROMOTE RELAXATION

In column A indicate how many times per week you engage in each activity. In column B indicate how frequently you would like to engage in each activity.

Active Relaxation Activities

	A	B		A	B
Sports	___	___	Stretching	___	___
Dancing	___	___	Yoga	___	___
Laughing	___	___	Sex	___	___
Walking	___	___	Other _____	___	___
Jogging	___	___			

Deep Relaxation Activities

	A	B		A	B
Massage	___	___	Deep muscle relaxation	___	___
Hypnosis	___	___	Progressive relaxation	___	___
Self-hypnosis	___	___	Mantras or sound focus	___	___
Autogenics	___	___	Breath focus	___	___
Biofeedback	___	___	Mandalas or visual focus	___	___
Guided imagery	___	___	Instant relaxation	___	___
			Other meditation _____	___	___

Passive Physical Relaxation

This includes massage, acupressure, physical manipulation and sexual activity. Touching is a basic human need, and some of the tension taking root in the body can be effectively discharged in this way. It also feels good.

What passive physical relaxation methods are a normal part of your life?

DEEP RELAXATION TECHNIQUES

Rest, diversions and active and passive physical activity alone are not enough to give most people the relaxation they need. Even after rest and strenuous exercise, deep tension can remain in our muscles. Our minds can still be filled with worries and unresolved feelings. We can become so accustomed to living with tension that we may not even be conscious that deep tension remains with us all the time.

Deep relaxation or meditation is an important part of stress management. If our lives are full of pressures, change and demands, attaining the rest and peace of meditation or deep relaxation seems almost a necessity.

A daily period of deep relaxation helps us in several ways. It discharges deep muscle and physical tensions, and helps us overcome anxiety and attain greater peace of mind. It teaches us to listen and be sensitive to the messages and needs of our bodies. It helps us to achieve greater energy, well-being and balance.

Cardiologist Herbert Benson of Harvard University, who helped conduct the most important psychological and physiological studies of the effects of meditation and deep relaxation, feels that the body has the capacity to attain a *"relaxation response."* This is the opposite of the stress response. Both the relaxation and stress responses are necessary to our lives, but each has its place. The stress response equips us for action and sustained high performance. We also have a need for regular periods of relaxation, where tension and stress are released.

Benson notes that the ability to trigger relaxation has been a part of almost every culture in history in various forms of meditation, self-hypnosis and guided mental imagery. Some cultures, like the Hindu and Buddhist religious traditions, evolved highly structured and complex systems for regulating the nervous system, for self-healing and for calming the body.

Our modern reliance on drugs, alcohol and food to tranquilize ourselves seems to have caused many of us to neglect the development of this natural skill.

Using deep relaxation, meditation, guided imagery or self-hypnosis, one can shut off a stress response that has been triggered in a crisis or after a demanding day. Or, one can train his nervous system to stay calm and not to react too drastically to normal stressors. This skill is another cornerstone of self-care: it enables us to immediately reduce the negative effects of stress, relieving many minor physical and emotional stress symptoms.

VARIETIES OF DEEP RELAXATION

Americans are attuned to brand names and different varieties; deep relaxation is no exception. Once we accept our need to learn deep relaxation, we are faced with a host of different methods, each competing for our attention. Are they different from each other? Which one is best?

Research is far from providing answers to these questions. However, it suggests that all the various types of deep relaxation and meditation have more similarities than differences. All techniques help us relax our outer muscles, deepen our breathing, and offer some focus for attention to quiet our minds. They are done sitting or lying in a quiet place, with attention focused inward. They all ask us to learn "passive attention"—paying attention to something without forcing, pushing or aiming at a particular goal or end point.

With those commonalities, each person can choose a method that fits his or her needs and personal style. Many cassette relaxation tapes offer guided imagery or music along with gentle instructions and suggestions. The varieties include:

- transcendental meditation
- deep muscle relaxation training
- autogenic training, which give suggestions to our body
- self-hypnosis.

Those who desire technology to help them, biofeedback offers second-to-second messages on how relaxed our bodies have become; biofeedback can be used to help us learn any method of relaxation.

MEDITATION

Meditation is an effective tool for relieving stress and tension and building calm and peace into your life. The meditative experience provides a model of what it feels like to be deeply relaxed. You will discover a mental/physical state of energy, calmness, clarity and warmth that is both self-empowering and pleasurable. The intention of meditation is to feel that way all of the time.

You can begin to practice relaxing and meditating by paying relaxed attention to *anything*—a word, sound, your breath, your body, or some positive-feeling state or activity. If your mind wanders, do not force it back to your object, but gently rein it in, back to what you are focusing on. Or, allow your mind to go where it wants, observing your own experience, watching but not adding your will to the flow of thoughts, memories and ideas. As you practice this passive style of attention, you will feel a sense of freedom and peace that comes from letting go or surrendering to the natural, spontaneous, inner process of meditation. It will become a way to contact deeper layers of yourself, an inner reservoir of energy and peace.

You will now learn some of the ways that you can relax or destress. The chief thing that you don't do is engage in characteristic thought patterns. In other words, don't think your usual thoughts in your usual way. Surrender them for a brief time knowing full well that they'll be waiting for you. The intention of meditation and relaxation is to quiet thoughts, to relax them and to let them go. This skill takes time and practice to learn, and it can be extremely difficult to do. Sometimes it helps to combine strenuous exercise with meditation. Any form of vigorous movement will usually enable you to sit quietly without thinking for a longer period of time than you're used to.

Some simple self-initiating ways to help quiet your mind include listening to music, following your breath, gazing at a crystal or flower, repeating a tone or sound. They all facilitate a physical state of deep relaxation.

EXERCISE 32 — BREATH MEDITATION

This is an easy way to begin your practice of meditation or deep relaxation. The exercise is adopted from simple forms of meditation. It consists of sitting quietly and comfortably, and paying careful attention to your breathing.

Sit in a quiet, secure environment. Close your eyes. Shift your attention from the outside world, and from your cares about your life, to your body and the physical sensations occurring right now. Notice as many sensations in your body as possible.

Pay attention to your breathing. In your mind's eye, imagine air going into your lungs as you inhale, going down deep into your abdomen, and then going out as you exhale. For a few minutes, just experience your breathing. If your mind wanders or you fall asleep, bring it back to your breathing.

As you inhale (through your nose if that is comfortable), count to yourself, "one." As you exhale, through your mouth, say "and." For the next breath continue your count—"two, and." When you get to four, begin again with "one, and." If you lose the count, start with "one."

Continue for ten to twenty minutes, or as long as you feel comfortable doing the exercise. Slowly open your eyes, and sit for a minute.

You can also meditate by selecting an object that attracts your attention. Sit quietly, spine erect, for ten or twenty minutes, gazing at the object. Give it your undivided attention. If a flower is before you, feel, taste and sense its shape, color and fragrance. Become the flower—dissolve into it. If distracting thoughts pass through your mind, accept them and let them go. Gently go back to the object of your attention, without pushing yourself. It will take a while to get used to this. After a session, you will feel relaxed, refreshed and rejuvenated.

GUIDELINES FOR DEEP RELAXATION

The following pages offer directions for several types of simple relaxation and meditation exercises. Make a commitment to practice them daily for a period of several weeks so that you can accurately assess their effects on your stress level and well-being.

Here are some general instructions for how to begin the regular practice of relaxation.

Daily practice

Relaxation is a form of physical training. It has no effect unless it is done regularly. Also, like any form of physical training, such as a sport, you have to learn how to do it. It is not a magic health cure for stress; it is a way of training your body to enter a deep, regenerative state. Some people can learn it quickly; others will take time, or need to work individually with an instructor.

For your initial practice allow enough time to learn something about relaxation. Do not attempt to assess its effects, or your own performance, until you have practiced it for two weeks. The effects may not be apparent until then. You may have trouble for the first day or two, such as finding it difficult to concentrate, or feeling some momentary increase in stress level or discomfort. Unless you develop some serious difficulty (this is rare), continue practicing.

Develop a routine

If you make a regular time and place to do your deep relaxation, you will be creating a habit that you soon will look forward to, and do automatically.

Keeping a chart for the first several weeks is a useful incentive and allows you to see graphically that you are making progress. Also, if you are learning in a class or from an instructor, you have a record to bring to class, so that you can discuss difficulties and problems. Use the Relaxation Log in Exercise 32, which you can fill out briefly before and after each of your relaxation periods.

An important part of developing a routine is to create a safe, protected place to relax. That means asking for help from the people around you, leaving your phone off the hook and doing whatever is necessary to ensure that you will not be disturbed. Create a special place, or part of a room, to do your exercise.

Time and posture

The best time to do a relaxation exercise is before a meal. Many people relax early in the morning and just before dinner. It can also be done after or during a stressful activity.

EXERCISE 33 — RELAXATION LOG

Before you start your relaxation, note in column 1 the stressful events in your day preceding your relaxation. In column 2 write down your prerelaxation S/R (stress/relaxation) level, using a subjective scale of 1–10 (1 reflects total relaxation, while 10 indicates being very highly stressed or tense). Put it after "before."

Do your relaxation exercise.

After the exercise, note your stress or relaxation level again, in the appropriate "after" location, using the 1–10 scale.

Then fill in some of the thoughts, feelings, body experiences, and/or other distinguishing occurrences during your relaxation period in column 3.

For week of: _____

A.M. RELAXATION

	Stressful Events of the Morning	S/R Levels 1–10	Experiences during relaxation: feelings, thoughts, etc.
MONDAY		Before ___ After ___	
TUESDAY		Before ___ After ___	
WEDNESDAY		Before ___ After ___	
THURSDAY		Before ___ After ___	
FRIDAY		Before ___ After ___	
SATURDAY		Before ___ After ___	
SUNDAY		Before ___ After ___	

P.M. RELAXATION

Stressful Events of the Evening	S/R Levels 1–10	Experiences during relaxation: feelings, thoughts, etc.
	Before ___ After ___	
	Before ___ After ___	
	Before ___ After ___	
	Before ___ After ___	
	Before ___ After ___	
	Before ___ After ___	
	Before ___ After ___	

The usual posture for deep relaxation is sitting straight in a chair, hands folded in your lap, feet flat on the floor. If you need back support, place a pillow behind you. You can also use a recliner chair, or even lie down, although these postures make it more likely you will fall asleep during the exercise.

Mental attitude

The mental attitude required for deep relaxation is opposite the mind-set required for most task-oriented activities. Sometimes it takes a while to become comfortable with the attitude of passive attention. Do not push yourself or try too hard to concentrate. Rather, let your attention focus on what you have decided to focus on—your breath, your muscles, a mental picture. If your mind wanders, simply finish the thought and bring your mind back to your object of attention.

Do not be critical of yourself or try to keep your mind from wandering. This will only defeat you and make you tense while you are trying to relax. Achieving a blank state of mind comes only after years of guided instruction and daily practice. Do not frustrate yourself with unrealistic expectations.

Passive attention has been described as paying attention to the process, rather than to the goal. Do not think about getting relaxed, which is your goal; pay attention to whatever sensation you are having at the moment. If you find it hard to do the exercise or to relax, pay attention to your body and try to find out why. You may need to finish a task before you are fully ready to relax.

Problems and discomfort

Because we all have expectations about the benefits of relaxation, many people begin to practice a relaxation exercise and feel they are not doing it right. It seems too simple! Their experience does not fit their expectations, however vague and unrealistic these expectations may be. In fact almost everyone is doing the exercise correctly. Trust yourself.

Sometimes a person will experience some discomfort, either physical tension or anxiety, during or after a deep relaxation exercise. This is because in relaxing you may become aware of tension in your body that you had ignored or not even realized, or you may be letting feelings or thoughts into conscious awareness that you had previously repressed. In most cases, the antidote is to wait for a while and then continue the exercise. However, if discomfort or anxiety persists, it is wise to work with an instructor until these reactions can be halted.

EXERCISE 34 — DEEP MUSCLE RELAXATION

Many people are not sensitive to the degree of tension that builds up in their muscles during a day of even quiet work. This exercise is designed to help you become aware of the difference between tension and relaxation in each of the major muscle groups. It also incorporates some of the suggestions that are part of autogenic training (e.g., heaviness and warmth in the arms, coolness in the forehead), which help to create the deep relaxation state.

Sit or lie comfortably, and close your eyes. Become aware of how tense or relaxed your body is. Pay attention to your body for a few moments.

Make a fist and tense your right hand (or your left hand if you are left-handed) for a few seconds, then relax and let it go loose. Then, tell your hands to become warm and heavy, and help the suggestion by imagining things like a heavy weight tied to your hand or the sun beating down on it.

Next, tense and relax your right forearm. Follow it up with suggestions and images for it to become heavy and warm. Do the same with your upper arm, shoulder, right foot, lower leg and upper leg. Your whole right side should feel relaxed, heavy and warm.

Repeat the procedure with your left side (or your other side). Your hands, arms, feet and legs should now be relaxed, heavy and warm. Wait for these feelings, or repeat the procedure again. It may take a few repetitions before you can do this. When you have mastered heaviness and warmth, you may be able to relax the muscles without having to tense them first.

Now, relax the muscles of your hips. Imagine that a wave of relaxation is passing up from your abdomen to your chest. Imagine the wave coming in as you inhale, bringing deep relaxation; then imagine the wave receding as you exhale. Do not tense these muscles. Tell your hips, your abdomen, and your chest to become heavy and warm. Let each breath become deeper, completely filling your abdomen. Wait for your breathing to become very deep before going on to the next stage of the exercise.

As you inhale, imagine that a wave of relaxation is continuing into your shoulders, to your neck, your jaw, your mouth, up to your face and to your scalp. Relax each muscle group in turn, imagining the relaxation passing over it. Pay special attention to the muscles controlling your eyes and forehead. (If you wear contact lenses, remove them before doing this exercise.) Now suggest to your brow to be cool; imagine a breeze or a cold compress touching your forehead.

Enjoy the feeling of deep relaxation. In your mind's eye, imagine that you are in a lovely, peaceful, relaxing spot, without a care in the world. Imagine the scene with all of your senses—feeling, hearing, smelling, seeing and even tasting what it is like to be in that special place.

When you are ready to finish the exercise, take two deep breaths, and open your eyes. Sit quietly for a moment or two.

EXERCISE 35 — BREATH AWARENESS

Sit in a balanced position. Settle into your chair so you feel as little strain as possible on your lower back or abdominal muscles.

Imagine a cord attached to the top of your head, pulling your spine perfectly straight and aligned from the top of your head to the bottom of your spine.

Move your feet around until they are both comfortably placed on the floor, approximately one and a half feet apart, with your calves perpendicular to the floor.

Lift your hands and drop them to your thighs. Now visualize the cord being cut; allow your head to move very slowly to a comfortable position.

Take a deep breath and gently and easily exhale. Allow your next breath to be the one your body takes itself, and watch your abdomen expand as you breathe in, and contract as you breathe out.

When you feel settled into your breathing, say to yourself on each in breath, "I am . . ." and on each out breath, ". . . relaxed." Allow your body to slip easily and comfortably into relaxation.

Continue this practice and soon you will be able to relax simply by taking a deep breath.

EXERCISE 36 — MUSCLE RELAXATION WITH GUIDED IMAGERY

This exercise can be done either sitting up or lying down. You might read the instructions slowly onto a cassette tape, and then play them back to yourself as you follow the suggestions.

Begin this process with the breath awareness exercise.

Slightly tense your hands, arms and shoulders. Concentrate on the tension and how it feels. Now very slowly begin to relax down through your shoulders, arms and forearms. Be aware of how it feels as you release the tension and replace it with relaxation. Relax your wrists, hands and fingers. Imagine this feeling of relaxation flowing downward through your body, all the way down to your toes. Pause.

Gently contract and tense your scalp, forehead, eyelids, the tissues around your eyes, your mouth and jaw muscles. Be aware of the tension. Slowly begin to relax your scalp, forehead, eyelids and the tissues around your eyes. Be aware of how it feels as you release the tension and replace it with relaxation. Relax your mouth muscles and jaw muscles. Now, using your creative imagination, imagine this feeling of relaxation flowing down through your neck, shoulders, arms and hands. Imagine this sense of relaxation going through your chest and abdominal area, down through your hips, legs, calves and feet, all the way to the tips of your toes. Pause.

Take a deep breath and tighten the muscles in your chest and abdomen, and then, while exhaling, allow your chest and abdomen to relax completely. Imagine relaxing your chest and abdominal area internally. Imagine all your organs, glands, even the cells, functioning in a relaxed, normal, healthy manner. Now tighten your hips, legs, feet and toes. Slowly begin to release the tension down through your hips, legs, calves, ankles, feet and toes. Pause.

Imagine that you have plugs in your big toes and that any tension remaining in your body is like water. Imagine that you have pulled these plugs and the tension begins to drain out of your toes. As it does, again imagine a deep sense of relaxation flowing from your scalp down through your forehead, eyelids, face and jaw muscles. Imagine this feeling of relaxation flowing down through your neck, shoulders, arms and hands. Allow this feeling of relaxation to flow downward throughout your chest and abdominal area, through your hips and legs, all the way down to the tips of your toes. Take a moment to imagine a state of mental and physical well-being and complete relaxation.

Give yourself ample time to come out of this state of relaxation. Before opening your eyes, and as you open them, flex your arms by bending them at the elbows and stretch them above your head several times.

EXERCISE 37 — GENTLE MUSCLE RELAXATION

Note: Because of the subtleness of this exercise, work only on one side of your body, preferably your dominant side.

Begin with the "breath awareness" exercise.

Throughout this exercise attend to your breathing and any other parts of your body that might be tensing unnecessarily. Pay special attention to your shoulders, your jaw muscles and your eyes. As you perform this exercise, tense only to the point where you notice the tension.

Bend the toes of your right foot under slightly. Hold on to this slight pressure while you examine your breathing and the rest of your body. When you let go, feel the entire right side of your body relax.

Lift your toes off the ground. Hold on to this pressure while you mentally examine your jaw muscles, your shoulder muscles, your eyes and your breathing. Very gently, allow your toes to come back to the floor and feel the entire right side of your body relax.

Push your heel down on the ground with just enough pressure to feel some slight tensing of your muscles. Repeat your check of body muscles and breathing. Very slowly, allow that tension in your calf muscles to go away. You will feel your right side relax even more.

Lift your heel off the ground and feel your thigh muscles slightly contract. Hold on to that tension while you mentally examine the rest of your body. Especially check your breath, keeping it calm and regular. See that you haven't clenched your teeth, and that your eyes are relaxed. Carefully allow your heel to come back to the floor and enter relaxation once again.

Pick your right hand up and bend your wrist toward your elbow until you feel your forearm tighten. Hold it while you check your shoulders and breathing, your jaw muscles and eyes. Gradually let it go, and feel your arm suffused with new energy and relaxation.

Bend your arm at the elbow to slightly tense your biceps muscles. Don't do a powerful demonstration, just enough to feel that slight muscular tension. This time, pay special attention to your shoulders; check to see that you haven't tightened up your right hand in the process. Check your breathing, your jaw muscles and your eyes. Then, let it all go, easily and gently.

Push your right hand down onto your right thigh, until you feel your triceps muscle tighten. Your shoulder will rise slightly, but your jaw and eyes shouldn't tense. Continue to breathe calmly and regularly. Hold on to that tension while the rest of you remains relaxed; then let go of that tension.

One final movement: lift your right hand and right leg and make small circles. Continue to breathe, and then let it all go.

Reeducating Your Stress Response

This practice will teach you to relax yourself deeply. It is a two-part exercise that will help you to become increasingly aware of the physical tension you are carrying and introduce you to a superb tool for instantly reducing stress—guided imagery.

Make sure that you will not be interrupted for several minutes. Sit or lie in any comfortable position. Most people are able to sit relaxed for a period of time when their spines are relatively straight. Back and neck support are helpful when sitting with your feet flat on the floor, and hands on the arm of the chair or in your lap. The exercise can also be done while lying down, but you run the risk of falling asleep.

Sit quietly for a few moments. Close your eyes gently. Become aware of all the sense impressions and feelings that arise from your body when you shift your awareness from the outside world to your inner world. Simply sit patiently and pay attention to your body. Hear what it says to you. You will be able to shift your awareness to different body parts and discover feelings that are ordinarily unconscious. Explore these bodily messages; they are important. They teach you the effects your life has on your body.

Let the following suggestions take root within you. If your mind wanders, or you fall asleep for a few moments, simply refocus and continue. Self-criticism and blame will only get in your way.

Take a long, deep breath, filling your chest. Allow the breath to flow deep into your abdomen. Hold your breath for a second or two. Exhale. You will feel an immediate relaxation and increasing awareness as you breathe fully and deeply. Follow your breath for a few moments, and see how this affects your body. Are you more relaxed? What changes have taken place?

Focus your attention on your arms and hands. Become aware of them. Explore the muscles in your arms, hands and fingers; see if there is any tension in them. If you discover tension, take a deep breath and imagine that your breath is moving from your lungs directly through your arms and hands, bringing with it a feeling of warmth and relaxation. Exhale and imagine that the muscle tension from your hands and arms is flowing out with each breath, leaving your hands and arms deeply relaxed.

Focus on your head, shoulders, chest, abdomen, back and spine, hips, buttocks and legs in the same manner. Remember to give relaxation suggestions for each part in turn.

Enjoy this relaxed state and the peaceful feelings that go along with it. Let each breath carry you deeper and deeper into the relaxation state.

Imagine seeing, feeling, hearing, smelling and tasting a place of beauty and peace where you feel completely relaxed. It may be somewhere that you once visited or a place that exists only in your imagination. Create this special environment for yourself as vividly as you can. What does it feel like, what do you see, hear, smell, taste? Do something with each of your senses. Relax and enjoy your special place.

Now, imagine that while you are there you are in a state of perfect, optimal health and well-being. What are you doing?
How do you feel? What do you look like? Enjoy the experience.

Slowly bring your attention back to the room, keeping with you the feeling of peace, relaxation and well-being. You can return to your personal relaxation and healing place whenever you wish. We recommend that you do so at least once a day.

EXERCISE 39 – STRETCHING AND BODY RELAXATION

Sit in a comfortable position. Allow your hands to hang down by your sides, and take in a full breath of air and exhale easily.

On your next inhalation, bring your head and torso easily erect. As you exhale, allow your head to fall gently forward. Continue breathing, directing your breath into the back of your neck. Inhale and bring your head to an erect position. As you exhale, slowly allow your head to fall backward. If you allow your mouth to open, your head can relax even more. Continue breathing, feeling any fullness or tightness in your neck. Breathe in and allow your head once again to come erect. Breathe easily and feel the degree of relaxation that you obtain from this simple motion when you do it with awareness.

Take another breath of air. Allow your right ear to fall toward your right shoulder. Exhale and breathe into the area that is stretching on the left side of your neck. Feel the tension in any of the muscles of your shoulders and neck. Slowly lift your right shoulder up toward your right ear. They may touch, but it isn't necessary that they do. Keep the motion easy and comfortable as your ear and shoulder come together. Hold this position for a moment.

When you feel ready, allow your shoulder to descend *slowly*, so you can experience your muscles letting go. You might feel some jerking in this motion. You may also notice that once you reach the area where your shoulder was when you began, you can now release it so that it drops even lower.

Slowly take another breath and allow your head to come erect. Breathe easily and feel the difference between your left and right shoulders.

Repeat on your left side.

Because most people experience their greatest amount of tension in the region of their shoulders and neck, do some neck rolls. Never jerk or force the neck. Always allow it to move much as if it were on ball bearings, going easily in a circle.

Begin by allowing your head to fall backward as you inhale. Slowly begin turning your head toward the left. As you head moves toward the front, begin exhaling, slowly and carefully watching your head move in this position. As your head begins to turn toward the right, begin to inhale toward the back position. Repeat this, inhaling as your head is in the rear position and exhaling as your head is toward the front. When you have completed two neck rolls in a clockwise direction, reverse the direction and do two neck rolls counterclockwise. Inhale and bring your head easily erect. Sit comfortably and feel your neck and shoulders.

Bring your arms in close to the sides of your body, and begin to raise your shoulders at the same time, as if you were trying to touch both shoulders to your ears. As you slowly exhale, allow your shoulders to come down. As they reach their lowest position, breathe easily, shake your hands just a little bit and gently move your shoulders.

Place your hands on the small of your back so that your thumbs are pointing toward your abdomen. Take a breath and lean backward, or arch your back a little bit to feel some tension in your abdomen. As you exhale, allow your torso to come forward. As you inhale, let your breath help to straighten you up. Repeat.

Allow your hands to position themselves on your hips. Breathe easily. As you exhale, stretch to the right. Inhale and come erect. Exhale and lean to the left. Repeat.

Raise your right leg, place your hands around your knee and leg, and pull your whole leg into your chest so you can feel some pulling on your lower back. Hold on to it for a moment, breathing into your lower back. Then allow your right leg to return to the floor. Repeat this on your left side, just pulling to that area where you feel stretching, but are still comfortable.

Close your eyes and sit quietly, listening to the sounds of your body. Hear and feel the silence within.

Notice the full flow of a breath of air at your nostrils. Watch the change of direction as you breathe out. On each inhalation say to yourself, "I am . . ." and on each exhalation, ". . . relaxed." Breathe in and out as you move into a deeper and deeper state of alert relaxation. Pause.

Discontinue all breathing exercises and simply watch the fullness of your breath, the continuous flow. Experience the silence between the in and out breaths.

Slowly begin to move your toes, your feet, your legs. Rock back and forth in your chair, move your shoulders, arms and hands. Easily turn your head and when you feel ready, take a full breath of air and open your eyes, feeling relaxed, rejuvenated and comfortable.

QUICK RELAXATION TECHNIQUES

There are a wealth of things that we can do when we are under stress. Some of the techniques suggested below are time-honored, and we have all used them. Others are new and we need to experiment with them and see how they work for us. Any of these techniques will work, provided we tune in to our needs early enough, and take action immediately.

Here is a list of quick relaxation techniques. You can add to the list.

- Take a five-minute break. Take a walk, sit or lie quietly; have a chat with someone.
- Take a short nap.

- Spend a few moments imagining a peaceful, relaxing scene or event in your life. Recall it in detail, imagining what it felt like with all your senses. Or imagine something pleasant that you are looking forward to doing in the near future, or something that you might do to reward yourself when the pressure or task is over.
- Massage your forehead, your eyes or the back of your neck. Learn some acupressure first-aid techniques.
- Deep breathing. Take a deep breath, letting it go deeply into your abdomen. Hold it for a few seconds and slowly exhale. This automatically sends a message to your body to relax.
- Do any deep relaxation technique for a few moments. Imagine your muscles relaxing.
- Run outside, or yell or scream for a few minutes if you can do it safely. Stretch your muscles actively to release tension.
- Switch to another job for a change of pace.

THE BIGGER PICTURE

When you began reading this book, you probably held the popular notion that burnout, stress management and personal effectiveness are qualities that belong to individuals. If you had a healthy personality, the benefits of education and natural skills, you would be good at managing stress and move away from burning out in the direction of peak performance.

Yet most of us maintain a funny contradiction in our thoughts. In addition to placing responsibility for stress management and peak performance on the individual, we tend to see stress and pressure as external forces that we are often powerless to prevent or to respond to effectively. We simultaneously make ourselves responsible for our performance, and see ourselves as powerless before the forces of stress and pressure.

As we reach the end of this journey, we come to another level and another way of looking at the whole area of performance. Everything—from stress to health to well-being to peak performance—depends not only on individual skill and efficacy, but on qualities of the work group, the environment and the organization.

In recent years, we have seen the birth of a new notion—or the resurgence of an old one—that the health, well-being and effectiveness of an individual are critically affected by the organization and the environment in which he or she works. It is difficult for an energetic and dedicated individual to avoid burnout and to excel in an organization that creates stress.

Thus, the focus of the search for balance is shifting from the individual to environments, organizations and contexts that promote these qualities. This does not devalue the role of personal power in creating change; visionary and peak-performing individuals have to work together to create the peak-performing organizations.

It is exciting to discover that the same qualities of empowerment, self-awareness, self-management, self-renewal and peak performance that characterize individual health can also be applied to organizations. Each quality and exercise that can be used by an individual or a work group can also be applied, with only a little adjustment, to an organization. Like a person, an organization, a family or a community is an organism that copes with pressure, adapts to change and maintains itself. It can do so in a healthy, adaptive way, or in a dysfunctional way. As organizations extend their search for personal excellence and well-being, they will begin to see themselves as an organism needing awareness, competence, power and nurturance to survive and thrive.

Appendix

ASSESSMENT TOOLS: HOW WELL AM I MANAGING STRESS?

Assessment Tools

The following eleven assessments are designed to help you evaluate your levels of stress in several areas of your life.

Each assessment scale will be placed on a continuum of:

- **Distress,** indicating difficulty,
- **Balance,** indicating that it is well-managed within your life, and
- **Hardiness,** indicating that it is an area of high performance and effectiveness.

At the end of each scale there is a place to total your score. Take your totals from each assessment and plot them on the summary graphs on page 175. These will allow you to evaluate, at a glance, the areas in your life that are overly stressful, balanced or controlled.

Keep in mind, as you plot your scores, that on some scales a high score indicates distress while on others a high score indicates hardiness.

Part 1 External Pressures

ENVIRONMENTS FOR STRESS

The following scales indicate pressures and demands in the two central environments in most people's lives. For each question, estimate the degree of pressure or demand that the situation places upon you.

A. Work and Career	Severe	Moderate	A Little	None
1. Too many tasks or responsibilities	(3)	2	1	0
2. Confused or ambiguous roles or expectations	3	(2)	1	0
3. Conflicting or competing demands	(3)	2	(1)	0
4. Conflict with supervisor or superior	3	2	(1)	0
5. Conflict or difficulty with co-workers	3	2	(1)	0
6. Dull, boring or repetitive work tasks	3	2	(1)	0
7. No rewards for work well done	3	2	1	(0)
8. Competition between co-workers	3	2	1	(0)
9. No opportunity for advancement	3	(2)	(1)	0
10. No room for creativity and personal input	3	(2)	(1)	0
11. No input to decisions affecting your work	3	2	(1)	0
12. Difficult commuting	3	2	1	(0)
13. Deadline pressure	(3)	2	1	0
14. Many organizational or job task changes	3	(2)	1	0
15. Difficult or distracting work environment	3	(2)	1	0
16. Loss of commitment or idealism	3	2	(1)	0
17. Confused or unclear expectations about tasks	3	2	(1)	0
18. Inadequate salary for your needs or expectations	3	2	1	(0)
19. Lack of friendships or communication with co-workers	3	2	1	(0)
TOTAL A	9	8	8	

(25)

B. Household, Family and Community	Severe	Moderate	A Little	None
1. Not enough money	3	2	(1)	0
2. Conflict with spouse	3	2	(1)	0
3. Conflict over household tasks	3	(2)	1	0
4. Problems or conflict with children	3	(2)	1	0
5. Pressure from relatives or in-laws	3	2	(1)	0
6. Household repairs	3	(2)	1	0
7. Not enough leisure time	3	(2)	1	0
8. Sexual conflict or frustration	3	2	(1)	0
9. Dangerous or stressful surroundings and neighborhood	3	(2)	1	0
10. Conflict or falling out with close friend or relative	3	2	1	(0)
11. Personal problem causing strain in family	3	2	1	(0)
12. No babysitters; difficult to get away from home	3	2	(1)	0

TOTAL B   10 5

(15)

JOB STRESS

	Almost Always	Frequently	Sometimes	Never
A. Work Environment				
1. My working conditions are hard on my body.	3	2	1	(0)
2. My work is dangerous or hazardous.	3	2	1	(0)
3. I feel pressure.	(3)	2	1	0
4. I am near toxic substances at work.	3	2	1	(0)
5. My workplace is bleak, uncomfortable or depressing.	3	2	(1)	0
TOTAL A		4		
B. Organizational Environment				
1. Office politics interfere with my work.	3	2	(1)	0
2. I can't get the information I need for my work.	3	2	(1)	0
3. What is expected or how to do things is not clear to me.	3	2	(1)	0
4. There is a competitive, backbiting atmosphere.	3	2	1	(0)
5. I don't have the resources I need to get my job done (e.g., time, money, help).	3	2	(1)	0
6. I do not participate in decisions that affect my work and job.	3	2	(1)	(0)
7. Things are changing too fast at work (new products, technologies, management team).	3	(2)	1	0
8. My work does not provide clear or reasonable pathways for advancement.	3	(2)	1	0
TOTAL B		9		
C. Job Role				
1. What is expected of me is not clear.	3	2	(1)	0
2. Too many things are expected of me.	(3)	2	1	0
3. I find myself being asked to do conflicting things.	3	2	(1)	0
4. I feel overloaded at work.	(3)	2	1	0
5. My job expectations are changing.	3	(2)	1	0
TOTAL C		10		

D. Self and Role Fit	Almost Always	Frequently	Sometimes	Never
1. I don't like what I do.	3	2	(1)	0
2. My job is boring and meaningless.	3	2	(1)	0
3. I have the wrong job for me.	3	2	(1)	0
4. My job doesn't utilize my skills and abilities.	3	2	(1)	0
5. I have ethical problems with what I do.	3	2	1	(0)
6. What I wanted/expected from my job has not turned out to be there.	3	2	(1)	0
7. I am not able to advance as much as I would like	3	(2)	1	0
8. I have been passed over for a promotion.	3	2	1	(0)
TOTAL D		7		

E. Interpersonal Environment	Almost Always	Frequently	Sometimes	Never
1. I have too much responsibility for other people.	3	2	(1)	0
2. Relationships between co-workers are poor or full of conflict.	3	2	1	(0)
3. Other people at work create conflict for me.	3	2	(1)	0
4. I am not clear where I stand—whether my work is respected by supervisors.	3	(2)	(1)	0
5. Too many people tell me what to do.	3	2	(1)	0
6. I am pressured by demands of clients/customers.	(3)	2	1	0
7. I have too much or too little contact with other people.	3	2	(1)	0
TOTAL E		8		

Part 2 Personal Health and Hardiness

NEGATIVE THOUGHT PATTERNS

The following statements reflect some general attitudes and ways of thinking that can add to or create stress and frustration.

A. Self-Criticism and Self-Doubt	Strongly Agree	Agree	Disagree	Strongly Disagree
1. I am usually critical of my own performance.	3	2	1	0
2. I make demands on myself that I wouldn't make on others.	3	2	1	0
3. I never think what I do is good enough.	3	2	1	0
4. I expect criticism from others for my work.	3	2	1	0
5. I get very upset with myself when things don't work out the way I expected.	3	2	1	0
6. When I am successful, I think I don't deserve it.	3	2	1	0
7. I don't think much of myself.	3	2	1	0
8. When something difficult arises, I find myself thinking of all the ways things can go poorly.	3	2	1	0
9. I often find myself in unpleasant situations that I feel helpless to change.	3	2	1	0
10. I often run into problems I can't solve.	3	2	1	0
11. I don't feel that I have much control over the events in my life.	3	2	1	0
12. Anxious and upsetting thoughts distract me when I am doing something.	3	2	1	0
TOTAL A				

B. Negative Expectations	Strongly Agree	Agree	Disagree	Strongly Disagree
1. I find it hard to hope for the best.	3	2	1	0
2. I expect the worst.	3	2	1	0
3. Other people rarely seem to come through for me.	3	2	1	0
4. I find it hard to look on the bright side of things.	3	2	1	0
5. I am a naturally gloomy person.	3	2	1	0
6. I have been continuously frustrated in my life by bad breaks.	3	2	1	0
7. My life is empty and has no meaning.	3	2	1	0
8. The future will probably not be as good as things are now.	3	2	1	0
9. I often seem to get the raw end of the stick.	3	2	1	0
10. Good fortune is mostly due to luck.	3	2	1	0
11. When things aren't going my way, I usually feel it is useless to try to change them.	3	2	1	0
12. Very little about life is fair or equitable.	3	2	1	0
TOTAL B				

COPING DIFFICULTIES

The methods of coping with stressful situations lead to difficulty when overused. Circle the number that most closely corresponds with how frequently you act that way in stressful situations.

A. Withdrawal	Often	Sometimes	Rarely	Never
1. I avoid challenges or new situations.	3	2	1	0
2. I am cautious and shy away from risks.	3	2	1	0
3. I try to forget difficult tasks facing me.	3	2	1	0
4. I find it hard to plan ahead and anticipate difficulties.	3	2	1	0
5. I find it hard to get involved in what I am doing.	3	2	1	0
6. I find minor tasks to avoid facing major ones.	3	2	1	0
7. I forget things I have to do.	3	2	1	0
8. I don't let myself get emotionally involved in things.	3	2	1	0
9. I fall asleep when things are difficult.	3	2	1	0
TOTAL A				
B. Helplessness				
1. Most of my stress seems to be unpredictable.	3	2	1	0
2. No matter how hard I try, I can't accomplish what I want.	3	2	1	0
3. I am not able to give what I want to those close to me.	3	2	1	0
4. I often find myself in situations that I feel helpless to do anything about.	3	2	1	0
5. I often run into problems that I can't solve.	3	2	1	0
TOTAL B				
C. Internalizing				
1. I keep my feelings to myself.	3	2	1	0
2. When I'm upset, I tend to hold it in and suffer silently.	3	2	1	0
3. I don't let anyone know I am under pressure.	3	2	1	0
4. I try to brace myself against pressure and stress.	3	2	1	0
5. I don't like to disagree with people.	3	2	1	0
6. When I'm upset, I avoid other people and go off alone.	3	2	1	0
7. I hold in my anger and frustration.	3	2	1	0
TOTAL C				

D. Emotional Outbursts	Often	Sometimes	Rarely	Never
1. When I'm upset, I blame someone else.	3	2	1	0
2. I blow up and let off steam.	3	2	1	0
3. I find that I easily become irritable.	3	2	1	0
4. I cry or fall apart emotionally and lose control.	3	2	1	0
5. I find myself angry.	3	2	1	0
TOTAL D				

E. Overcontrolling	Often	Sometimes	Rarely	Never
1. I try never to be late for appointments.	3	2	1	0
2. I am rushed.	3	2	1	0
3. I get impatient when I have to wait.	3	2	1	0
4. I try to do everything myself.	3	2	1	0
5. I don't have time for hobbies or outside interests.	3	2	1	0
6. I worry about things before I do them.	3	2	1	0
7. I rarely take time for myself.	3	2	1	0
8. I always put other people before myself.	3	2	1	0
9. Other people let me care for them.	3	2	1	0
10. I don't get much satisfaction from my achievements.	3	2	1	0
11. There is never enough time to get things done.	3	2	1	0
12. I can't start a project without thinking of another one facing me.	3	2	1	0
TOTAL E				

F. Type A Behavior	Often	Sometimes	Rarely	Never
1. I try to be on time for all appointments.	3	2	1	0
2. I find it hard to find time for personal errands.	3	2	1	0
3. I am faced with irritating and frustrating situations.	3	2	1	0
4. I eat rapidly and finish meals before other people.	3	2	1	0
5. I find myself doing several things at one time.	3	2	1	0
6. I give everything I have to my work.	3	2	1	0
7. I like to be the best at whatever I do.	3	2	1	0
8. I get impatient when someone is taking too long at a job I could do more quickly.	3	2	1	0
9. I tend to keep my feelings to myself.	3	2	1	0
10. I am very ambitious.	3	2	1	0
11. I have few interests outside of work.	3	2	1	0
12. I want my worth to be recognized by the people around me.	3	2	1	0
13. I hurry even when I have plenty of time.	3	2	1	0
14. I set deadlines for myself.	3	2	1	0
15. When I am tired, I tend to keep pushing myself to finish a task.	3	2	1	0
16. I am hard-driving and competitive.	3	2	1	0
17. I am precise about details.	3	2	1	0
18. I think ahead to the next task.	3	2	1	0
19. I tend to get angry when I am in situations beyond my control.	3	2	1	0
20. I let other people set standards for me.	3	2	1	0
TOTAL F				

ACTIVE COPING

This exercise assesses the degree to which you utilize active coping strategies. For each statement, circle the number indicating how frequently you employ that type of behavior when confronted with a problem.

	Often	Sometimes	Rarely	Never
A. Support Seeking				
1. Find someone to delegate it to.	3	2	1	0
2. Share it with someone.	3	2	1	0
3. Talk to others about it and share feelings.	3	2	1	0
4. Seek information from others.	3	2	1	0
5. Try to find someone who knows how to handle it.	3	2	1	0
6. Talk it over with someone you trust.	3	2	1	0
7. Seek advice and support of friends.	3	2	1	0
8. Talk problem over with counselor or doctor.	3	2	1	0
9. Share it with the family.	3	2	1	0
TOTAL A				
B. Diversion/Tension Release				
1. Decide it's not worth worrying about.	3	2	1	0
2. Do relaxation exercises.	3	2	1	0
3. Do active physical exercises.	3	2	1	0
4. Look at the humorous side of it.	3	2	1	0
5. Go away for a while to get perspective.	3	2	1	0
6. Reward or indulge yourself when finished.	3	2	1	0
7. Decide it's not really your problem.	3	2	1	0
TOTAL B				

C. Direct Action	Often	Sometimes	Rarely	Never
1. Take extra care to do a good job.	3	2	1	0
2. Finish the job immediately.	3	2	1	0
3. Do as good a job as possible under the circumstances.	3	2	1	0
4. Think it through and try to change your viewpoint or way of looking at the situation.	3	2	1	0
5. Put it in its place; don't let it overwhelm you.	3	2	1	0
6. Anticipate and plan ahead to meet challenges.	3	2	1	0
7. Make several alternate plans.	3	2	1	0
8. Let people know about angry or uncomfortable feelings.	3	2	1	0
9. Let people know the task is too much or you are too busy.	3	2	1	0
10. Negotiate so that the task is more manageable.	3	2	1	0
TOTAL C				

SUPPORT NETWORKS

This exercise assesses the quality and level of support in your life of the three major networks: family, friends and work. After each statement, circle the number that best describes how true each statement is for you, as you are feeling now.

A. Family (or Intimate) Support	Very True	Somewhat True	Slightly True	Not True
1. My family members (or intimate friends) take time for me when I need it.	3	2	1	0
2. My family members (or intimate friends) understand when I am upset, and respond to me.	3	2	1	0
3. I feel accepted and loved by my family.	3	2	1	0
4. My family allows me to do new things and make changes in my life.	3	2	1	0
5. My spouse (or partner) accepts my sexuality.	3	2	1	0
6. My family gives me as much as I give them.	3	2	1	0
7. My family expresses caring and affection to me and responds to my to my feelings, such as my anger, sorrow and love.	3	2	1	0
8. The quality of the time I spend with my family is high.	3	2	1	0
9. I feel close and in touch with my family.	3	2	1	0
10. I am able to give what I would like to my family.	3	2	1	0
11. I feel I am important to the people in my family.	3	2	1	0
12. I feel that I am honest to the people in my family and that they are honest to me.	3	2	1	0
13. I can ask the people in my family for help when I need it.	3	2	1	0
TOTAL A				

B. Friendship Support	Very True	Somewhat True	Slightly True	Not True
1. I usually place the needs of others above my own.	3	2	1	0
2. I feel I give more than I get from people.	3	2	1	0
3. I find it difficult to share my feelings with other people.	3	2	1	0
4. I am not able to give what I would like to other people.	3	2	1	0
5. I don't feel cared for or valued by the people around me.	3	2	1	0
6. I usually can't find people to spend time with me when I want to.	3	2	1	0
7. I am often lonely and alone.	3	2	1	0
8. I find it hard to ask for what I want.	3	2	1	0
9. I don't usually feel close to other people.	3	2	1	0
10. There are few people I can really count on.	3	2	1	0
11. Few people know me very well.	3	2	1	0
12. People don't seem to want to get to know me.	3	2	1	0
13. I tend to hide my sexuality or feel uncertain about it.	3	2	1	0
14. I find it hard to touch other people.	3	2	1	0
15. Other people rarely touch or hug me.	3	2	1	0
16. I find it hard to ask other people for help.	3	2	1	0
17. I am always doing things for other people.	3	2	1	0
18. People rarely help me.	3	2	1	0
19. When it comes down to it, I feel that I am basically on my own.	3	2	1	0
20. I have few friends or people I am close to.	3	2	1	0
21. I don't like to spend time with other people.	3	2	1	0
22. I feel distant and apart from other people.	3	2	1	0
23. I don't expect much from people.	3	2	1	0
TOTAL B				

C. Work Support	Very True	Somewhat True	Slightly True	Not True
1. When I run into trouble, there are co-workers I can seek out for help.	3	2	1	0
2. The people around me care about me as a person.	3	2	1	0
3. I feel I can ask questions and negotiate with supervisors about work assignments.	3	2	1	0
4. I am clear about what I am to do and what others expect from me.	3	2	1	0
5. I am not usually afraid that co-workers are critical of me behind my back.	3	2	1	0
6. People at work are more concerned about getting things done than about competing among themselves.	3	2	1	0
7. There are people I talk to each day informally.	3	2	1	0
8. I feel my abilities are valued by others at work.	3	2	1	0
9. Information is shared freely among people who should know things.	3	2	1	0
10. When I can't do something on my own, I can take my problems to others and they will help.	3	2	1	0
11. I can ask for guidance and help from superiors.	3	2	1	0
12. The climate of my workplace is pleasant and comfortable.	3	2	1	0
13. When people are upset about something at work, they usually talk about it.	3	2	1	0
14. Many things about work are pleasant and enjoyable.	3	2	1	0
15. People are given what they need to complete the tasks they are assigned.	3	2	1	0
16. I have outlets to help me handle the frustrations and irritations of my work.	3	2	1	0
TOTAL C				

MEANING AND LIFE PURPOSE

This exercise looks at how you approach living, and how you see your future and the meaningfulness of your life, work and relationships.

	Strongly Agree	Agree	Disagree	Strongly Disagree
1. I am not involved in my work.	3	2	1	0
2. My work is not very meaningful or satisfying to me.	3	2	1	0
3. My work feels routine and boring.	3	2	1	0
4. There are few challenges and creative tasks in my work.	3	2	1	0
5. I am not very involved with my family.	3	2	1	0
6. My family life is not very satisfying or meaningful to me.	3	2	1	0
7. I am bored and disinterested in my family life.	3	2	1	0
8. My life is rarely challenging and exciting.	3	2	1	0
9. Nothing much is new or unpredictable in my life.	3	2	1	0
10. My life does not have a central purpose or goal.	3	2	1	0
11. My life does not seem to meet many of my deepest needs.	3	2	1	0
12. My life is taken up with burdens and responsibilities.	3	2	1	0
13. There is not much that I look forward to in my life.	3	2	1	0
14. I do not feel that there is any higher force or guiding purpose evident in humanity.	3	2	1	0
15. I do not feel that I have lived up to my potential or lived as creatively and successfully as I might have.	3	2	1	0
TOTAL				

PERSONAL WELLNESS CHECKLIST

To estimate your degree of wellness, check how often each of the following is true for you.

	Almost Always	Often	Sometimes	Almost Never
1. I awake each morning feeling refreshed and energetic.	3	2	1	0
2. I feel that I can get what I want out of life.	3	2	1	0
3. I enjoy my family relationships.	3	2	1	0
4. I know that other people care about me.	3	2	1	0
5. My body is flexible and full of energy.	3	2	1	0
6. I enjoy regular exercise.	3	2	1	0
7. I eat nutritious and well-balanced meals.	3	2	1	0
8. I have good, reliable friendships.	3	2	1	0
9. There are people in whom I can confide.	3	2	1	0
10. I like the way my life is going.	3	2	1	0
11. I am working toward my life goals.	3	2	1	0
12. I am able to manage the stress in my life.	3	2	1	0
13. I am involved in my work and find it meaningful.	3	2	1	0
14. I do not smoke.	3	2	1	0
15. I avoid overuse of alcohol and drugs.	3	2	1	0
16. I know how to have fun.	3	2	1	0
17. My body is a source of pleasure to me.	3	2	1	0
18. I take good care of my teeth and the rest of my body.	3	2	1	0
19. I express my creative and spiritual selves.	3	2	1	0
20. I know that I can get what I need from others.	3	2	1	0
TOTAL				

STRESS SYMPTOMS

Check how frequently you have experienced each of the following symptoms of distress over the past month.

	Nearly Every Day	Every Week	Once or Twice	Never
1. Muscle tension	3	2	1	0
2. Back pain	3	2	1	0
3. Headaches	3	2	1	0
4. Grinding teeth	3	2	1	0
5. Stomach ache or upset	3	2	1	0
6. Heartburn	3	2	1	0
7. Vomiting	3	2	1	0
8. Diarrhea	3	2	1	0
9. Constipation	3	2	1	0
10. Abdominal pains	3	2	1	0
11. Colds, allergies	3	2	1	0
12. Chest pains	3	2	1	0
13. Skin rashes	3	2	1	0
14. Dry mouth	3	2	1	0
15. Laryngitis	3	2	1	0
16. Palpitations	3	2	1	0
17. Tremors or trembling	3	2	1	0
18. Twitches or tics	3	2	1	0
19. Dizziness	3	2	1	0
20. Nervousness	3	2	1	0
21. Anxiety	3	2	1	0
22. Tension and jitteriness	3	2	1	0
23. Keyed-up feeling	3	2	1	0
24. Worrying	3	2	1	0
25. Unable to keep still	3	2	1	0
26. Fear of certain objects, phobias	3	2	1	0

	Nearly Every Day	Every Week	Once or Twice	Never
27. Fatigue	3	2	1	0
28. Low energy	3	2	1	0
29. Apathetic—nothing seems important	3	2	1	0
30. Depression	3	2	1	0
31. Fearfulness	3	2	1	0
32. Hopelessness	3	2	1	0
33. Crying easily	3	2	1	0
34. Highly self-critical	3	2	1	0
35. Frustrated	3	2	1	0
36. Insomnia	3	2	1	0
37. Difficulty awakening	3	2	1	0
38. Nightmares	3	2	1	0
39. Accidents or injuries	3	2	1	0
40. Difficulty concentrating	3	2	1	0
41. Mind going blank	3	2	1	0
42. Forgetting important information	3	2	1	0
43. Can't turn off certain thoughts	3	2	1	0
44. Loss of appetite	3	2	1	0
45. Overeating, excessive hunger	3	2	1	0
46. No time to eat	3	2	1	0
47. Overwhelmed by work	3	2	1	0
48. No time to relax	3	2	1	0
49. Unable to meet commitments or complete tasks	3	2	1	0
50. Withdrawing from relationships	3	2	1	0
51. Feel victimized, taken advantage of	3	2	1	0
52. Loss of sexual interest or pleasure	3	2	1	0
TOTAL				

TENSION MANAGEMENT ACTIVITIES

Indicate how much of the time during the past month you have utilized each of the following activities to cope with your daily tension.

	Every Day	Once or Twice a Week	A Few Times	Never
1. Smoking	3	2	1	0
2. Alcoholic beverages	3	2	1	0
3. Overeating	3	2	1	0
4. Sleeping	3	2	1	0
5. Television	3	2	1	0
6. Fights with family members	3	2	1	0
7. Angry emotional outbursts	3	2	1	0
8. Tranquilizers	3	2	1	0
9. Aspirin and other pain killers	3	2	1	0
10. Prescription drugs	3	2	1	0
11. Marijuana, cocaine, etc.	3	2	1	0
12. Ignore or deny stress symptoms	3	2	1	0
13. Withdraw from other people	3	2	1	0
14. Criticize, ridicule or blame other people	3	2	1	0
15. Create conflicted personal or sexual relations	3	2	1	0

TOTAL

PART I - External Pressure

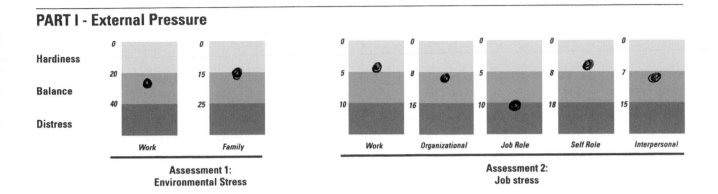

Hardiness
Balance
Distress

Work · Family

Assessment 1:
Environmental Stress

Work · Organizational · Job Role · Self Role · Interpersonal

Assessment 2:
Job stress

PART II - Personal Style of Stress Management

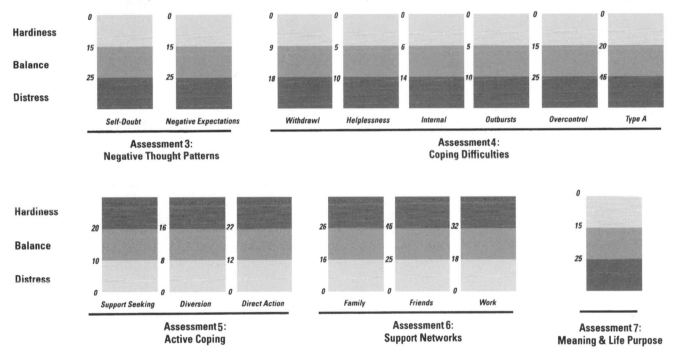

Hardiness
Balance
Distress

Self-Doubt · Negative Expectations

Assessment 3:
Negative Thought Patterns

Withdrawl · Helplessness · Internal · Outbursts · Overcontrol · Type A

Assessment 4:
Coping Difficulties

Hardiness
Balance
Distress

Support Seeking · Diversion · Direct Action

Assessment 5:
Active Coping

Family · Friends · Work

Assessment 6:
Support Networks

Assessment 7:
Meaning & Life Purpose

PART III - Personal Health and Hardiness

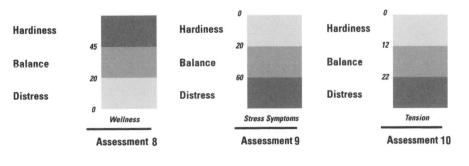

Hardiness
Balance
Distress

Wellness

Assessment 8

Hardiness
Balance
Distress

Stress Symptoms

Assessment 9

Hardiness
Balance
Distress

Tension

Assessment 10

About the Authors

Drs. Cynthia Scott and Dennis T. Jaffe are senior partners of HeartWork, Inc., a San Francisco-based organizational design firm. The firm provides consultation training programs and keynote presentations to assist organizations in the development of an empowered workforce.

Dr. Scott earned her Ph.D. in Clinical Psychology from the Fielding Institute. She is the author of nine best-selling books. Dr. Jaffe holds a Ph.D. from Yale University. He has authored a dozen books. Together they have written several management books including *Managing Organizational Change, Empowerment,* and *Organizational Vision, Values and Mission.*

If you enjoyed this book from Crisp Publications, please write or call for a free catalog.

1200 Hamilton Court
Menlo Park, CA 94025-9600
1 (800) 442-7477